Advance Praise for *Flip the Switch*:

"Strategy without communication is just theory. What Dianna delivers in Flip the Switch is a playbook for leaders to align their inner voice with their outer influence. She bridges purpose and persuasion, showing how clarity of message can ignite clarity of action - for yourself and those you lead. As someone who trains executives to speak with impact, I see Flip the Switch as a masterclass in leading with courage, connection, and conviction."

— Dr. Laura Sicola, Bestselling Author & Keynote Speaker; Executive Communication and Influence Coach

"Flip the Switch is a powerful call to action for leaders at every stage of their journey. Dianna combines lived experience with practical wisdom to show how courage, clarity, and empathy can transform not just organizations, but people's lives. A timely and inspiring guide for leading in today's era of uncertainty."

— Kathleen Taylor, Chancellor, York University; Chair, Atlas Partners, Element Fleet and The Hospital for Sick Children; Former President and CEO, Four Seasons Hotels and Resorts; Former Chair, Royal Bank of Canada

"Flip the Switch is a powerful reminder that growth begins when we dare to step beyond comfort. Dianna's insight on building an 'inner cabinet' especially resonated, as my own career has been shaped by mentors and advocates who opened doors. What makes this book stand out is that it's not theory—it's lived experience. Though written from a woman's perspective, its lessons hold universal value for any leader striving to succeed and make lasting impact."

**— Paul Martin, Chief Operating Officer,
Lawrie Insurance Group**

"Dianna's book cuts to the core of modern leadership. Flip the Switch urges us to overcome fear and lead with intention, fostering environments rooted in trust, empathy, and excellence. It's a powerful read that resonates deeply, shaping you as both a leader and an individual."

— Darci Walker, President, The Brick

"This book doesn't just inspire - it sparks real conversations. Dianna's personal stories are the heartbeat of Flip the Switch. From bias to envy she gives voice to truths we often struggle to name and then provides a framework to rise above them. For leaders in logistics and beyond, this is a guide to navigating complexity with clarity and courage."

— Andreea Crisan, President & CEO, Andy Transport

DIANNA FIORAVANTI

Flip the *Switch*

From Playing it *Safe...* to *Crushing* It!

Unlock Your Free Flip the Switch Self-Assessment

Before you dive in, I want to give you something that will make this book even more powerful for you—a tool designed to meet you exactly where you are and help you see what's possible next.

The Flip the Switch Self-Assessment is your personal starting point. It reveals where your energy is aligned, where it's leaking, and which parts of your **6P Model—Person, Purpose, Passion, Playbook, Perseverance, and Partnership—**are ready for a breakthrough.

Readers who complete the assessment before or during the book gain faster clarity, deeper alignment, and a far more personalized experience. It turns the pages ahead into a mirror, a roadmap, and a partnership—so you're not just reading… you're transforming.

Think of it as your first switch, the moment you stop guessing and start leading your life with intention.

Download your free assessment at:
https://fliptheswitch.diannafioravanti.com

Dedication

Dedicated to my daughter Alexis

To my dearest Lexi,

This book carries your spirit in every page.

Since you were a little girl, you've inspired me with your quiet courage, your authentic voice that rises when it matters most, and your perseverance in the face of challenge. You have a lightness that fills every room and a playful energy that brightens the world around you, even when no one's watching.

In the most beautifully imperfect way, you remind me every day of the incredible power of possibility, of what it means to begin again, to stay curious, and to believe in magic that can't always be seen but can always be felt.

May you always lean into your superpowers to flip the switch when life calls for it and keep it lit when things get hard. May you also never stop dreaming big, laughing loud, and leading with that radiant heart of yours.

You're my living joy, my greatest teacher, and the legacy I'm most proud to carry. Thank you for being my muse, my mirror, and my daily reminder of the joy in simply being all you were meant to be.

Stay inspired always, with all my love,

Mom

PS. I love you most.

Contents

Foreword

Genuine leadership is often discussed, but it's rarely demonstrated with the intensity and impact Dianna brings to every role she holds. Throughout her executive career (spanning the insurance industry, international logistics, and high-performing sales organizations), she's led with a deep commitment to self-awareness, character, and human connection.

Dianna has stepped into organizations in moments of uncertainty and listened to understand the truth of the team experience (not to confirm assumptions). Her leadership is based on relationships. From speaking with frontline workers while walking the floor of a distribution center at 6:00 a.m. to inviting critical voices into boardroom meetings, she builds trust through action and being present while remaining humble and grounded.

During a time of organizational change, while others may have focused solely on operational alignment, Dianna prioritized the cultural and emotional impact on employees. She established open forums, influenced leaders, created a shared experience between teams, and mentored the frontline leaders through the transition. Because of her efforts, performance metrics exceeded expectations, and employee trust scores rose when most organizations would have experienced sharp declines on the "change curve."

Dianna releases the untapped capacity hidden in all teams.

Repeatedly, she's shown that leadership is about supporting and connecting with others, even when the prevailing culture prizes control. For Dianna, earning trust and holding tight to the belief that people perform at their best when they feel seen, respected, and challenged is what makes her leadership style stand out as powerful and real.

She has a unique ability to rally people around a shared purpose. In an insurance organization, Dianna led a company-wide reset of the customer-experience strategy by co-creating solutions with cross-functional teams, turning away from the typical top-down mandates commonly used in business.

Under her leadership, outcomes consistently and measurably improve. Employee and customer engagement scores increase and retention stabilizes. And perhaps most impressively, shareholder value grows through long-term focus on people and purpose. Unsustainable cost-cutting tricks have never been an option for Dianna.

In this book, she shares what so many of us have experienced firsthand: that leadership grounded in character supports the culture while also being good for business. Dianna doesn't dwell on the basics like financial literacy, perseverance, or critical thinking (even though she embodies all of them). Instead, she shows us how vulnerability, emotional intelligence, moral clarity, and the courage to lead without ego differentiate outstanding leadership.

It's an honour to introduce this work and the remarkable leader behind it.

James Wood, past President, Kuehne + Nagel Canada.

Author Introduction

*"Some people want it to happen, some wish it
would happen, others make it happen."*
— *Michael Jordan*

GEM: One choice...one moment...can change the course of your entire life.

But What If...

...the pull toward something extraordinary keeps colliding with the comfort of what's familiar, and that moment to "make it happen" keeps slipping by?

That was me. The woman who knocked down doors without blinking suddenly choosing safety instead.

It happened at exactly 5:33 p.m. on a bright March afternoon; the moment my daughter was born. In that breath, adventure gave way to protection. My world shifted from "What's next?" to "Is she safe?" I went from chasing possibility to guarding what mattered most.

Safety became my compass. Safety meant she was protected. Safety meant I was too. But that same safety would one day become my mountain I'd have to climb to find myself again.

We don't realize how often our need for safety quietly shapes our choices. It disguises itself as being "responsible" or "practical" or the "right thing to do." And for many of us, especially women, this pull toward safety can be magnetic, even if we don't label it.

It shows up in the silent moments: the job we stay in, long after it stops inspiring us because the paycheck feels like protection. The meeting where we stifle an idea burning in our mind because speaking up feels too risky. The relationship we keep trying to fix because familiarity feels safer than freedom. The dream we keep tucked away on the back shelf until "someday" because everyone else's needs come first.

Safety can be comforting…until it starts costing us pieces of ourselves.

GEM: Self-awareness is your golden ticket! It turns the light back on inside you.

Maybe you're there too, standing at the edge of change, caught between what feels safe and what feels right. If so, you're not alone. Leaders, teachers, students, dreamers; so many of us live in this space, asking the same question: *Am I ready?* But it isn't just fear that holds us back. It's the weight of uncertainty. And uncertainty isn't going anywhere. In fact, it's one of the few things we can count on in the world we live in today.

Aside from the numbing (and sometimes paralyzing effects) of uncertainty, it can also serve as the silent hope that there "might" be more out there, so we find peace in waiting on that *hope*. And if that's not enough, we combine the hope with that voice in our head whispering, *"We're not enough."* And what do we do next? We settle. We choose safety. We play small. We let dreams fade without realizing it.

The stories we tell ourselves in these moments often feel protective, but they become the handcuffs that hold us back. But there's *real hope* in all this. You hold the key. And the moment you decide to see your story differently, you can *Flip the Switch* and change everything.

> ***GEM: You're standing at the brink of transforming your life, and the only thing between you and the future-you is the power of Flipping the Switch.***

GEMs: My Personal "Aha" Moments

GEM stands for Growth, Empowerment, Momentum. These are my personal nuggets of wisdom. They're the lessons that lit my path through some of life's darkest hours, arriving as unforgettable "aha" moments that changed everything. Each is a treasured insight (like a precious jewel) shaped by experience and polished by reflection.

You'll find GEMs throughout this book, tucked into stories and reflections. My wish is that they ignite something special in you; a spark of growth, empowerment, and momentum you can return to anytime you need to flip your own switch.

My Story

Twenty-five years ago, I was single, bold, and unstoppable. I chased every opportunity because I could. I broke through glass ceilings, saying yes to risks that scared the hell out of me and flipping the switch without even realizing it.

I often raised my hand for roles that looked impossible on paper, the kind that made me feel nauseous and excited simultaneously. I boldly applied and got creative on how I would execute the role once I had it—I was resourceful. I made choices in personal relationships that often didn't fit the mold, but I kept moving forward because I believed I was built to grow.

Looking back, some of the most defining moments of my life didn't happen in boardrooms. They happened in my personal life. The choices that shaped me the most were the ones other people judged harshly, especially against the backdrop of my Catholic upbringing. Some saw them as unthinkable, even disappointing. But despite what the naysayers thought, those decisions weren't made from rebellion. They were about protecting myself and my daughter and became investments in the future I envisioned for us.

I carried the weight of those decisions like luggage I didn't remember packing. I felt I'd failed as a daughter, a woman, a mother, and a leader. Guilt became my safety blanket, replaying the same story until I couldn't see my reflection anymore. And at some point, truth came calling on me, and it hit hard: the only one holding me back was me! The only way through was to get out of my own f&%king way—and flip my own damn switch!

As painful as they were, those choices taught me the power of self-awareness and the freedom of self-acceptance. They became the weight room where my perseverance muscles were built. And I had to keep showing up and working those muscles every day.

GEM: The greatest unfinished project you'll ever work on is you.

Every day, I chip away at this unfinished project called me. With every book I read, every conversation I have, every connection I intentionally make, every decision I choose, and every moment of reflection I take, I'm shaping the me of tomorrow. And authenticity is at the center of it all.

The most surprising part of this messy, uncomfortable, yet liberating journey was stumbling into one of the most unexpected truths of my life. It may sound simple, but stay with me, because it opened a whole new world of possibility: it's okay to be me. Just me.

Damn right it is! I don't need to be perfect, because perfection doesn't exist. I don't need to be polished, because what does that even mean? And by whose definition? I just need to be my real self.

I show up stronger and more present when I stop chasing the myth of perfection, stop listening to that nasty inner critic and just show up as myself. My family, friends, and colleagues don't need another mask of expectation. They need me fully there, fully real. The idea of perfection had to go from my vocabulary and from my frame of mind.

**GEM: Being fully, unapologetically,
imperfectly me can get messy, but it's real.
And real is exactly who I'm meant to be.**

And when I finally unwrapped the full gift of self-awareness (not just peeked at it, but really owned it), another truth struck me: failure was never my enemy. I just had to flip my switch and see it differently. Every time I stumbled, missed the mark, or watched a dream slip through my fingers, I learned lessons deeper than success could ever offer. Failure, it turns out, wasn't holding me back. It was pushing me forward.

**GEM: Failure isn't your enemy. It's
been your fiercest ally all along!**

Once I made the first big flip in my personal life, I found the rhythm to keep my life in motion, and the misalignment in my professional world became impossible to ignore. I'd preached growth while quietly choosing safety. How could I have let that happen? On the surface, my insurance career spanning two decades was on fire! But inside, I was on autopilot, leading from the sidelines instead of the core of my purpose.

I'd already rebuilt my life once through courage, self-trust, and telling myself the truth. And it was time to do it again. This time, not just for me, but for the people I led.

I began paying more attention to my leadership. How was I showing up? How was I impacting the business, our people, and our customers? What was my superpower, and how could I magnify it?

I soon discovered something was different about me: I lead with quiet power. I created impact without the spotlight, without the loud voice, and without the show. I quietly connected, I influenced, and I created a ripple effect of positive energy that was contagious—all anchored to my values and my purpose.

Results were at their best when my focus stayed on leadership and development, when I poured into people instead of just strategy. Creating a culture where others felt seen, psychologically safe, and genuinely connected was so much more than my "job." It was my rhythm and my joy. Watching people rise, not because they had to but because they wanted to, reminded me why I do this work. *That* is my superpower.

But I still wondered, *could that be it?* Was it really that simple? I didn't want to lead teams; I wanted to transform them. I didn't want to just make an impact; I wanted to multiply it. I craved a bigger stage for my reach to serve more people, tell more stories, and turn more inner lights on. I needed to take what I'd learned about leadership, trust, and courage, and do what I do best but on a bigger scale.

My second big flip happened on a beautiful Saturday morning while talking with my daughter. I told her to dream big—so big that it would scare her! She grinned and leaned in. "What's *your* big scary dream, Mom?"

The question stopped me cold. The mirror had turned, but I didn't have an answer for her. I'd been urging her to live boldly while I'd quietly chosen safety.

Her words lit a fire I couldn't ignore. I wanted more. I wanted a bigger environment to serve and a bigger purpose to live. So, I did what I teach now. I flipped the switch! I moved industries, raised my hand for a bigger role, and became the first female president of Kuehne + Nagel Canada, a move that didn't just reignite my career but also reignited *me*.

That's where *Flip the Switch* was born. Out of the risks, failures, wins, and wake-up calls. Sometimes, the exact moment you've been putting off is the one that changes everything once you finally embrace it.

GEM: Sometimes the bravest thing you can do is answer the same question you ask of others.

I wrote *Flip the Switch* because I know what it feels like to let safety win over potential. In these pages, you'll uncover six core superpowers—the 6Ps—that fuel authentic, purpose-driven leadership. Supported by two core principles (the R.E.A.L. Leadership Truths and the H.E.R.S. Trust Model), the 6Ps are your playbook for development, connection, and courage, and the tools to flipping the switch and keeping it on.

Put your potential back at the top of your priority list by uncovering your own unique superpowers and give yourself permission to use them boldly. Use this book to see what I also had to face, that the old story ("I'm not enough") was never mine to carry. The real story is, "I was made for this," and so are you.

Flip the Switch is about real-life experience. It's about energy. It's about learning how to convert the doubt, fear, and negativity that weighs you down into fuel that powers you forward in all areas of life. Peel back the layers that keep you small and step into the version of you that's waiting.

At the core, my purpose has always been to create environments where people thrive. And that purpose is alive in this book. Every page is a space for you to dream bigger, risk more, and believe in yourself fully. My role is simply to guide using the blueprint I've built through experience. The Flip the Switch method and the tools I share are to help you make the small, daily shifts that create extraordinary breakthroughs.

What to Expect from Flip the Switch

My Personal Reflections:

I'll share a lot of deeply personal reflections and real experiences, but to honour the privacy of those involved, some names, timelines, and specific details have been intentionally adapted or withheld. I've written this book from a place of honesty and integrity, and I want to be as open as possible while respecting the journeys of others.

My Asks:

This book will only work if you do the work. So, here's what I ask of you:

— **Think big and move bold:** Don't play small with your life. The bold moves you were born to make are waiting on you.

— **Un-piss yourself:** If you're stuck in old habits, caught in negativity, or resisting the uncomfortable work it takes to grow, call yourself out and choose differently.

— **Step from comfort into courage:** This journey will push you. Push forward when the stakes are high, because that's where the real growth and reward lives. Risk forward.

— **Build your own playbook:** I'll share the tools and stories that reignited my passion and purpose. Take them, adapt them, and design your own strategy so you can lead yourself and create environments where others thrive too. Playing it safe won't get you to your North Star.

— **Turn the ordinary into extraordinary:** Failure isn't your enemy. Let it teach you and fuel your momentum. Close the door on complacency for good.

— **Commit to reflection:** Keep your journal close while reading. Capture your thoughts, track your breakthroughs, and honor your story as it unfolds. You're the architect of your story, and the one you've created until now is your greatest teacher. Listen to it.

— **Let your brilliance shine:** You're not here to blend in. You're not here to play it small or safe. Unlock what makes you unique and live fully in the life you were made for.

My Heartfelt Promise to You:

Together, we'll do the work. Nothing happens overnight, just like there is no "easy button" or magic pill to win the Stanley Cup or turn your body into a lean, powerful machine. What creates lasting change is showing up repeatedly with intention. That's what we'll do here.

Along the way, doors to opportunities you may not have noticed before will open. Your confidence will grow. And most importantly, you'll uncover the superpowers you've had all along. Your authenticity (imperfections included) will become the very thing that you're most proud of.

I'll provide practical tools you can start using immediately. They'll help you build your own strategy, bringing the future-you to life faster than you thought possible. Whether you're just starting out, leading at the top of your field, or somewhere in between, these tools will accelerate your development and stay in your toolbox for life.

Your power isn't "out there." It's already in you. *Flip the Switch* will show you how to ignite it through the six superpowers you already have within you. And together, we'll unleash them.

If you're ready to break free and meet your future self, this is your moment. Regardless of whether this book found its way to you through purchase or as a cherished gift, you're here because you're ready to leap from the ordinary to the extraordinary. This is your moment to design a future built from your unique brilliance.

It's game time; not the safe game, but the one where you bet on yourself. Welcome to the bold path where anything becomes possible.

GEM: Today is the perfect day to begin uncovering the imperfect and remarkable you.

CHAPTER 1

Un-Piss Yourself.

"We become what we think about."
— Earl Nightingale

GEM: Your life follows your dominant thoughts. Change your thoughts, and you change your story.

It's time to un-piss yourself. It's the moment to stop playing small and fire the voice inside that keeps you safe, stuck, and swirling in doubt. The one whispering, *"You're not ready," "You're not smart enough," "You're not strong enough."* That voice isn't protecting you. It's parking you at a price you can't afford.

Your future doesn't need perfection. It needs you, honest, present, and in motion.

Name the Enemy

Modern life can be exceptionally loud with headlines, group chats, calendar pings, and email notifications. And it's when the noise turns up that our inner critic drops its favourite remix: "You can't," "You won't," "Who do you think you are?"

If you've been feeling heavy or scattered, you're not broken. You're merely caught in a spiral of thoughts that won't quit and makes it hard to find the light leading to the way out.

Humans have around 60,000 thoughts every day. And of those, 75% of those thoughts are negative, and 95% of those negative thoughts are repetitive (Loder 2023). It's like our brains are running a 24/7 pessimism podcast! The question is, how do we turn those around to be more positive, new thoughts?

The good news is you hold the switch! And when you cut the noise, you make room for the voice that knows you. The voice that's capable, powerful, and ready to step into more of "you." So, will you become someone who actually takes ownership and flips the switch? Someone who becomes available to yourself, so you can own your own life?

Most people aren't lazy. They're just stuck. And being stuck feels like a waiting room where life is happening on the other side of the door, but instead of walking toward it, you're glued to your phone, scrolling the same social media feed on repeat. Deep down, you know you should get up and boldly push open that door, but it feels easier to just sit there and wait for an invitation to step in.

Take a breath. What are you thinking about right now? Is that thought fueling you or draining you? Either way, you can shift it. And when you shift even a degree or two, your story starts to tilt toward possibility.

What I Mean by "Un-Piss Yourself"

What did you feel when you saw the title of this chapter? Were you curious? Put off? Did you perhaps think, "Dianna, really?" like my dad did? Good! That spark is the point. I chose the title because it's what I've said to myself in stairwells and parking lots before big moments. It's a life skill they never taught us in school, but after today, you'll use it everywhere.

What if you really could flip a switch to un-piss yourself? Like a lightbulb turning on in the middle of a negativity swirl? Imagine grabbing that mental lever and yanking yourself out of self-doubt and all those tired, old stories that keep you stuck. Suddenly, you're back in motion and fueled understanding and purpose. No manual required, no "settings" to fix. Just one clear option: *un-piss yourself.* The moment you do, the negativity that feels taller than you starts to crumble, like a wall coming down one swing at a time.

> **Un-piss yourself:** The art of energy conversion. It's turning negative charges into forward motion in sixty seconds or less.

It's a big, bold switch right in front of you. And flipping it doesn't mean pretending things are fine. It's about spotting the energy leak, closing the tap, and taking one honest step forward. Why waste this fuel? Use it to lift you.

"It takes more energy to be negative than positive" (Lepins, n.d.). Think about that for a second. It's actually easier for you to soar than sit around being pissed!

The most difficult part isn't the flip but catching the swirl early, spotting the leak before it drains you. Once you master this, the flip will become natural.

The Un-Piss Yourself Flip

1. **Pause**. Take 5 slow breaths. Feel your feet. Drop your shoulders.

2. **Name it.** In one sentence: *I'm spiraling(swirling) about _____ because _____.*

3. **Flip it.** Choose one:

    a. Movement: stand up, walk the hallway, stretch, do 5 squats or the best dance move you can do.

    b. Music: one power song that changes your state instantly. Have it at your fingertips to play (anytime, anywhere).

    c. Mantra: I can't, therefore I must (say it out loud).

4. **Micro-win.** Choose the next best step. Ask yourself: What moves me forward by 1% right now? What will advance my purpose? Do that. (E.g., send the hard text, book the call, draft the first paragraph.)

Got it? Here's the 60-second drill if you need a quick flip:

— 0-10s: Pause (in for four, out for six)

— 10-25s: Name it (the swirl and the trigger; out loud)

— 25-45s: Flip it: Pick one option to move (movement, music, mantra)

— 45-60s: Micro-win (commit to one next step and start it)

The Pause Button (and Why It Matters)

The first move isn't push. It's *pause*. Pausing is how you aim:

— **Your body resets.** Your breath lengthens, your shoulders drop, and your nervous system gets the important message: *we're safe enough to choose.*

— **The pattern breaks.** The negative swirl of thoughts loses grip. You create space between what triggered you and how you'll react. That space is golden.

— **Your values aim in.** Your purpose gets the spotlight here. Ask yourself, what decision would I be proud of a week from now?

GEM: Pause doesn't slow you down. It aims you.

The Review That Changed Everything

I remember the hallway more than the room. The carpet was worn. The fluorescent lights had that faint buzzing sound, or maybe the buzz was in my head (that famous inner critic). I clutched a folder I didn't need, already building my defense: the missed targets, a culture I was trying to flip from fear to trust, losing our top sales producer and the hit that came with it, shifting strategy midstream while rebuilding a boutique brand in a market that wasn't sure who we were anymore. It hadn't been "a year." It had been more of a street fight.

My boss was the President of the firm, a sharp thinker known for his quick wit. What was most memorable was his yearly Wet Head award. It went to the person who stuck their neck out most. Sometimes, the risk blew up, but sometimes, it broke new ground. And either way, it took guts, and that effort was rewarded.

My heart pounded as he asked the question I feared most. "So, tell me what went well this year, Dianna?" My mind went completely blank, and the silence was deafening. The voice in my head, though, was louder than ever. *Nothing went well. You should have done more. You should have seen it coming.* I wanted to disappear into the floor.

But as I was ready to crumble, he leaned in with a smile. "Let me tell you what I saw in your leadership this year." Surprisingly, he didn't mention numbers. He talked about perseverance, the steadiness when things got ugly, the way I kept the team moving when it would've been easier to quit. He said, "You didn't make excuses. You led."

The room shifted and felt brighter. My shoulders dropped. My breath came back. I sat up straighter. Nothing outside of me had changed, but I did. Recognition does that. It lets you breathe again.

Then I only heard two words from his next sentence. "Wet Head." I'd achieved that year's award for mental toughness. I'd stuck my neck out and held the line when it would've been easier to hide.

That day, I learned the power of courage and what that power can do when you keep showing up.

After that meeting, I snuck out of the office through the back entrance for some air. I kicked off my heels and sat on the cold concrete step. I cried for a full minute, from relief, release, and gratitude. I then texted my husband: *He saw me. Not crazy. I'm going to be okay.* I wiped my face and wrote these lines in my notes app: *Connect the culture. Rebuild the brand. Lead with heart and hustle.* After, I stood up and went back to work.

I learned a critical lesson in life and in leadership that year: in moments of crisis, leaders are graded first on steadiness and energy. Results matter, but your state will drive them.

That's what gave birth to the un-piss yourself switch. The moment you catch yourself swirling in negativity, call it out and choose differently. Instead of sitting in the stink of a poopy attitude (as my 5-year-old daughter used to call it), flip the switch to clear the air, step back into your stronger self, and move forward with intention.

GEM: Recognition isn't a trophy. It's fuel.

Mantra: "I can't; therefore, I must" (and How I Use It)

This line was ingrained into me from a very young age, on the sidelines of baseball games, at piano recitals, and often during late-night study sessions. Whenever I said, "I can't," my parents (especially my mother) would say, "therefore you must." At the time, it felt almost like a punishment, but as an adult, I understand how important that statement is. It helped to move me from feeling helpless to helpful.

When life gets tough and situations become uncertain around me, I reflect on the lessons instilled in me from a young age and look into the future with a bold and optimistic lens.

My parents were loyal in their belief that quitting was never an option. They often reminded me to reframe my thoughts when feeling like I couldn't do or achieve something.

GEM: "I can't; therefore, I must."

I use this phrase often to flip my state and create a micro-win because it converts emotion to motion. It doesn't demand a miracle, but it forces me to move.

Here is your template: *I can't ___, therefore I must ___ because ___.*

Some practical examples that may help you put this into practice:

— *I can't fix the whole quarter; therefore, I must rebuild trust with three key clients by Friday, because trust - not tactics - is what turns a quarter around.*

> — *I can't control their decision; therefore, I must state our value with clarity and confidence, then walk away clean because self-respect sets the tone for every future partnership.*

> — *I can't do everything today; therefore, I must finish the one thing that moves us 1% forward because momentum - no matter how small - is how I win the long game.*

GEM: Courage grows through repetition, not through speeches.

Sometimes flipping the switch isn't a big external move. It may be in those quiet, private moments when you feel completely exposed, questioning your worth and wondering if you've got anything left to give. That's when it matters most.

Talk to Your Future Self

When the soundtrack in your head starts the negative swirl, talk to your future self. This secret strategy has proven itself to me for over a decade. I'm not referring to the nay-saying neighbour or the inner critic we're trying to un-piss. I'm talking about the future-you who's achieved the life you've always wanted.

I literally talk to her every day. It sounds odd, but that's how it works. She's a lens that's different from the one I typically have when the moment strikes. Talking to her puts my identity back in charge. Future-me is the version of me who's already lived through this and kept her integrity. She's not full of drama, and she knows what matters most to me.

Flip Tool: Talk to Future You

- "Future me, what do you need from me right now that you will thank me for?"

- "If this were happening to someone I care about, what would I tell them to do?"

- "What's the one move that keeps us honest and moving today?"

Write the answers down. That's how to develop and maintain momentum.

On the hardest days, I make it tangible. I write a ninety-second note on my phone that starts with, *Dear Future Me*, and ends with three lines I can keep: a truth, a boundary, and a next step. Always write down the next step to ensure you make a commitment.

Sometimes she gives me the nudge I need: "Stop the swirl, Dianna. Pause. Un-piss yourself. Flip the damn switch, and for goodness' sake, move!"

Practicing this self-talk turns it into muscle memory. It's what steadies me when emotions run high and stakes feel heavier than logic.

Before a hard conversation with a teammate who'd been poisoning the culture, I walked out of the boardroom and into the stairwell to un-piss myself. I hit pause: I put a hand over my heart and took five slow breaths. I named it, then for the flip, I asked future-me, "What do you need from me right now?" The answer was simple, and one that may ring true for you too. *Be clear. Be kind. Be done.* I went back into the boardroom, spoke plainly, protected the team, and for the first time in weeks, slept through the night.

GEM: Future-you is counting on you to do the hard work today.

Anne

In the 1950s, a young couple welcomed their daughter into the world. Like all parents, they dreamed of a bright future for her. But when she turned two, their joy was overshadowed with worry. She hadn't spoken a single word.

Doctors confirmed a truth no parent wants to hear: Anne was deaf with only about 20% hearing in one ear. Her parents were faced with a decision that would shape her entire life. They could send her to a school for the deaf, where she could communicate openly through sign language, or they could place her in a mainstream school where she'd have to lip-read and adapt to a world not built for her. After long nights of soul-searching, they chose the harder road. From that point on, Anne's eyes became her ears, and her heart became her guide.

School was a challenge. Surrounded by classrooms full of noise and chatter, Anne worked tirelessly to piece lessons together by reading lips and watching faces. Her speech carried the mark of her hearing loss, but her determination was fierce. She learned to play the piano and drive a car, and she graduated from university with honors.

Anne had one big dream: she wanted to become a teacher. So, in 1972, with excellent grades and unmatched persistence, she applied to teacher's college. She was full of hope, but the response broke her heart. She was rejected purely because of her disability.

The message was clear: *you're not enough.*

Many of us know what that feels like. To be dismissed. To be told, directly or indirectly, that we don't measure up. Anne felt it, too. But instead of wallowing, she flipped the switch and built a 38-year career in insurance, and her leadership, skill, and fortitude made her disability barely noticeable.

But as she neared retirement, her dream of teaching returned, and Anne tried again, this time with the Insurance Institute of Canada. And she was accepted. Not only did she teach, but in 2013, she was named Instructor of the Year! Rejection and what seemed like limitations became Anne's redirection.

Anne is my mom, and her perseverance shaped me. When the world said "no," she built her own "yes" and taught me to do the same.

GEM: You're not defined by the label. You're defined by your response.

Who Are You in the Storm?

Mental toughness isn't just about weathering the storm or turning a red light into a green light. It's about finding the courage to dance in the rain. What a beautiful flip in thought, finding joy and a way forward in an otherwise chaotic mess. And unbeknownst to me, in so many ways, my mom taught me how to do this.

Storms are always part of the deal, no matter what climate you live in. Markets shift, people disappoint, and plans blow up, and the timing is never polite. You don't get to pick the weather either, but you *do* get to pick your posture.

Power begins the moment you stop bargaining with reality and ask with honesty, "Who am I going to be in this?" It's not about being polished like the perfect social media post. Who is the you who keeps your word to yourself when no one is watching? Feel your feet on the floor, unclench your jaw, let your shoulders drop and your breath catch up with you. Tell the truth about what's actually happening and what matters right now, then choose your identity first and your action second.

GEM: Real power is born not from avoiding the storm but from deciding who you'll be inside it.

When the Heat is On

When I walked into that company for the first time, I thought I was ready. It was a new role and a big opportunity, with the usual mix of ambition and optimism. But within five days, reality hit hard. It was frozen in time. The office was a museum of old habits: stacks of paper and printed emails everywhere. And the leadership was stuck in a control-and-command era where fear ran deeper than trust.

My predecessor thought the best way to introduce me was a printed Facebook photo thumbtacked to the bulletin board with the words, *here is your new boss.* That was it. No conversation, no connection nor any form of proper introduction. Just a photo on a wall, and it certainly set the tone for what was ahead.

The mandate was clear on paper: grow the business, beat the market, and build alignment with the parent company and global network. But what I quickly learned was that none of those relationships were healthy. Everything was siloed. The infrastructure was crumbling, contracts were outdated, and the biggest shock came just months in, when our most seasoned sales rep (the one holding the largest portfolio) walked out. The financial impact was immediate and painful.

I was crushed. Every day felt like a battle I wasn't sure I could win. I questioned myself constantly. *Did I make a huge mistake? Do I really have what it takes?* The weight of it was exhausting, and failure felt closer than success.

In one of my darkest moments, I leaned on my husband Stephene. "Dianna," he said, "you aren't a quitter." It was so simple, yet it was that reminder combined with my mother's voice in my head (*I can't; therefore, I must*) that gave me the push I needed. It was time to un-piss myself, flip the switch, and turn the chaos into an opportunity.

The next morning is when the magic started, all because I decided I wasn't going to do it alone. I called on my inner cabinet, the people I trusted most, and with their counsel, I built a plan rooted in the most important question I've ever been asked: *What is the legacy you want to leave here?*

That question changed everything.

I started small but intentional with weekly coffee chats to create transparency, monthly sales meetings to rebuild connection, quarterly engagement events to break silos, and regular recognition moments to show others that they mattered. We tied operational excellence to clear KPIs and celebrated improvements, big and small. We layered in automation, redefined the brand in the market, and slowly rebuilt trust with the parent company and global network. It was about progress over some unachievable idea of perfection. And it was messy.

But over time, something shifted. The fear that once defined the culture gave way to connection as the silos began opening, and the people who'd been disengaged started standing taller. And years later, one of the managers I worked shoulder-to-shoulder with became the leader of that very company, which is still thriving today. That's the power of fortitude, collaboration, and a clear playbook—the quiet kind of power that builds cultures.

Looking back, I call this period: "the era of Paper Walls and Coffee Chats." It taught me that true leadership isn't a quick fix, and how you show up truly beats a polished strategy every day. You need to show up even when the room is cold, speak from the heart, and choose progress, because perfection doesn't exist.

The unknown will get messy along the way, but messy just means you're moving. Messy means you're alive and growing. Messy is the new sexy. So go ahead: get messy, get sexy. Flip that switch, un-piss yourself, and soar!

GEM: The playbook matters, but the posture wins.

Mental Toughness in High Heels

Perseverance and staying positive are always choices, and when life throws its hardest tests into your path, those choices matter most. No one's immune to setbacks or the moments that shake our confidence. But even in the toughest situations, we get to decide how we show up. And choosing to move forward with strength and optimism might not erase the hardship, but it changes the outcome.

At a time when women weren't yet seen as leaders to bet on, when breaking in as game-changers was still the exception and not the rule, the choice to stay the course was everything.

Back then, the corporate world didn't leave much room for feelings, struggle, or truth. Vulnerability was a weakness, empathy was irrelevant, and motherhood was something you managed quietly behind the curtain. If I was late because I'd dropped my daughter at childcare, that was frowned upon. If I left early for her school play, that wasn't "on trend." My male counterparts had stay-home partners who covered that ground, but for me, finding a balance demanded constant negotiation.

So, I played the game. I booked full vacation days for thirty-minute performances and smiled through the guilt, worried that if I showed too much humanity, I'd be seen as less committed and less promotable. But I didn't waste energy dwelling on the inequities. I just un-pissed myself and kept moving. My daughter and my future self were counting on me. That didn't make the injustices I faced right, but it fueled my determination to work hard enough (and smart enough) to create change and to impact lives in a way that felt real and true.

And today, because I didn't give up on me, I get to show up as I am now. This is my time. Every day, I have the privilege to lead, to shape culture, and to influence change. Every day, I take steps my future self dreamed about. The vision in my playbook never stops calling, and opportunity meets me there because that's where my focus is. I un-piss myself and keep moving forward.

Tony Robbins says, "Where focus goes, energy flows" (Robbins 2024). Choose to direct your focus where it matters most: possibility, growth, and impact.

Resilience Rewired...
My Flip the Switch Mantra

(Copy, borrow, or steal—please!)

I'm the architect of opportunity. I don't wait. I create.

*I'm a leader who seizes the moment, even
when the moment feels impossible.*

I'm the discoverer of possibility in places others overlook.

I'm the igniter of action, not just for myself but for those I lead.

I'm strong, grounded, and purpose driven.

*I face every challenge with courage and intention
because my future self is counting on me.*

*"What's the one move that keeps us honest
and moving today?"*

Your environment plays a significant role in shaping you. It can provide the energy, incentive, and inspiration you need to move forward. Surrounding yourself with positivity can be a game-changer for your personality and lifestyle. Reflect on the company you keep, because there's immense opportunity waiting for you when you align yourself with the right people.

GEM: You're the driver. And sometimes you just have to get out of your own f*&king way!

Your Pocket Flip-Kit: 3 Key Takeaways

1. *Un-piss yourself (state before strategy)*

You can change your state in 60 seconds. Pause, name the swirl, pick a lever (movement/music/mantra), then choose your micro-win by taking the next 1% step.

2. *Pause to aim, then choose who you'll be*

The pause isn't a stall; it's how you aim. In the space you create, decide who you'll be in the storm, then let that identity set your tone and your move.

3. *Borrow from future-you (and use the mantra)*

Talk to future-you for understanding and courage. Ask, "What's one move I'll be proud of tonight?" If you hear, *I can't*, answer with, "therefore, I must" and turn it into a small, honest action.

Flip the Switch Moment

Now it's your turn to flip the switch. Take a pause here to reflect. This is where insight becomes transformation. We learned a lot about fortitude and the importance of un-pissing yourself to truly unleash your potential. Grab your journal, and for ten minutes, let's have a quick chat.

1. **Name the waiting room**. Where are you stuck right now? Give me one sentence. What instantly came to mind for you?

2. **What's the cost of *not* flipping?** List 3 costs (to your health, money, relationships, career, impact, etc.) and make it sting.

3. **Pick your flip.** Movement, music, mantra, future self; what will make you move? Do it for 30 seconds.

4. **What is your micro-win, aka your next best step?** What advances your purpose by 1% today? Start or schedule it now.

CHAPTER 2

The Art and Method of Real Change

"Almost every significant breakthrough is the result of a courageous break with traditional ways of thinking."
— Stephen Covey

GEM: Every bold move starts the same way, with your stomach in knots and your soul telling you, "Do it anyway."

We all have those times when everything feels like it's falling apart before the day even begins. For me, it was 7:42 a.m., and I was already running late—half-dressed, coffee spilled, laptop screaming for updates. My morning was chaotic, and so was my mood. Then I stopped mid-rant, looked in the mirror, and laughed. *Flip.* The situation didn't change, but I did.

In its simplest of forms, that's the art of flipping the switch; catching yourself in the spiral and choosing a different energy.

Flipping the switch isn't magic. It's a method. It's the art of noticing, naming and choosing, again and again, until courage becomes your default setting, then using the tools that already reside inside of you to keep that switch turned on.

The art unfolds something like this:

1. Noticing what triggers your fear or hesitation.

2. Naming the truth and what's really holding you back.

3. Choosing differently, especially when it's uncomfortable.

That courage never waits for permission. It's built in the quiet hours when no one's watching, in the late-night arguments with your own self doubt and those private moments when you decide that the status quo is just too small for who you're becoming.

True transformation never happens where it's comfortable but when you dare to disrupt. It grows when you re-imagine what's possible and lead from a place that's deeply authentic (and often wildly uncomfortable).

How do you know when you're making progress? Those wins are earned behind the scenes through the work done when no one's clapping and there's no audience to impress. That's where you flip the switch.

GEM: The spotlight doesn't make you shine. The work you do in the dark does. Greatness grows in the unseen moments when no one's watching.

Congratulations on arriving here! You've decided to stop letting the story of "what's been done to you" run your life and start owning what you do next. You've chosen to un-piss yourself, leaving behind what no longer serves you and step into something more intentional, courageous, and real!

Part 1: The Art of the Flip

Who Are You When No One is Watching?

Growing up, my dad would say that the hours spent training when the stands are empty are the ones that win the game. Meaning, the work you do when no one is watching is what shows up when the lights come on.

Every winter, we'd train: me throwing two hundred, sometimes three hundred, pitches a day in a cold church hall while my friends were out doing anything but that. I complained, I argued, I tried every negotiation tactic I knew. But Dad would just say, "It all depends on how bad you want it." And that was that. Because I wanted it badly enough to do the invisible work.

The same rule applies to everything that matters. The diet you fudge on, the hard conversation you postpone, the boundary you keep promising yourself you'll hold—all of it. What you avoid doesn't just sit there quietly waiting for you to come around. It steals from you.

And in my world, avoidance is theft. Every time you dodge the hard thing, you steal from your own becoming.

I like to use the KISD principle (keep it simple, Dianna): What you resist, rules you until you face it head-on.

GEM: The best things in life (the magic, breakthroughs, and peace) wait on the other side of that tough decision or uncomfortable conversation.

Only you can show up as you, for you. It's your number one job. Flipping the Switch starts with personal awareness, the kind that becomes the heartbeat of your life. It's the ability to show up as your most authentic self when there's no audience, no likes, no emoji's, no witnesses. Because if you can be that person when no one is watching, imagine how unstoppable you'll be when they are!

GEM: Discipline is rent, and game day is the receipt.

And when you can't see your own progress anymore, borrow the eyes of your inner cabinet (the people who keep you honest, grounded, and brave). Ask them what they notice shifting in you. Sometimes their mirror is the clearest one you'll find, because even when you're doing the work alone, you aren't meant to do it in isolation. Behind every bold flip is an inner cabinet, and make no mistake, they don't do the repetitions for you, but they make sure the repetitions matter. They remind you of your "why" when you start bargaining with it.

The Table that Builds You: Your Inner Cabinet

One of the secrets to truly un-pissing yourself is getting comfortable reaching out for support. We think strength means handling everything alone, but real strength is knowing when to link arms for connection and collaboration. Sometimes the fastest way to get unstuck is to stop doing it all by yourself.

There's power in viewing collaboration as a superpower, one you can nurture, call on, and practice every single day.

GEM: When extraordinary and beautiful minds come together, they create an unstoppable force where magic isn't just possible but inevitable.

Flipping your mindset from solo survival to collaborative strength will ground you, especially when frustration or disappointment try to take you out. Reaching out might come naturally to some, but for most of us, it's a skill we need to practice.

One of the most powerful tools is my inner cabinet. It's the circle of people I can rely on, always. They keep me honest and real. Picture a group of your most trusted allies sitting around a metaphorical kitchen table, similar to Michelle Obama's *The Kitchen Table* (Obama 2018). Unlike in corporate boardrooms or Zoom calls, it's a place like the one from your childhood where life actually happened, unfiltered, unpretentious, and beautifully messy. That's your Inner Cabinet. The people who see you—your brilliance, your blind spots and your breaking points—and love you through it all.

That table is where courage is built. It's a place of both refuge and recalibration. Each member brings their own flavour of wisdom through different experiences and different strengths, all contributing to a shared purpose: helping you flip the switch on what's next. Together, they ensure you show up as the highest version of yourself.

GEM: Your inner cabinet is your lifeline. Choose them with care, and they'll carry you higher than any title ever could.

Though don't get it mistaken; this inner cabinet isn't about having hundreds of names on a list or a massive LinkedIn network. It comes down to quality, not quantity. It's the boutique collection of voices that matter most. The mentors, colleagues, and friends who've earned the right to speak truth into your life. The ones you call not just when you win but also when you're stuck.

Take a moment to think about your lifelines. Not executives in suits or people performing for attention, but your inner circle of builders and believers. This is your personal launch pad, the handpicked crew who challenge you, champion you, and call you out when you start dimming your own light. Their titles don't matter, but their truth does.

Inner Cabinet Cue: Quick Check In

- Who sees you practicing when no one's watching?

- Who'll tell you when you're drifting from your truth?

- Who reminds you of your greatness when you forget?

Keep those names close. They're your fuel for every flip.

The Ignition Point

When you show up as you, for you, it's authenticity to the core. Authenticity, to me, is raw self-awareness; awareness of your values, your beliefs, and your behaviours wrapped up and presented as you to the world. It's the ignition point for all things possible. It's having the guts to stand in the mess and still be seen. It's the quiet consistency that builds trust, showing up real every day, imperfect and grounded in your truth. When you can lead from that place, that raw core, that's where transformation begins.

> ### *GEM: Authenticity alone doesn't make you a leader, but leading with authenticity is at the heart of R.E.A.L. leadership.*

Once you're truly aware—aware of who you are, how you got here, and who you want to become (or unbecome)—you'll know exactly when to make shit happen, to be who you were always meant to be. You'll move from safety to *crushing it,* just by learning how to flip the switch.

Flipping the switch doesn't happen in comfort zones. It's born in the fire where those tough, messy, and even toxic moments shake you awake. If you've ever had an "enough is enough" moment that pushed you into motion, you know exactly what I mean. What may have looked like chaos was actually an opportunity quietly waiting beneath the surface; the ignition point where uncertainty meets possibility.

The Interference

You're standing right there, on the edge of a bold move, completely self-aware and ready to flip the damn switch, when out of nowhere, it happens: the interference.

It's not always loud. Sometimes, it's subtle, and many times, it's wrapped in authority or love. But when it hits you, it usually hits like fire (and not the positive kind). It could be a toxic boss, a manipulative friend, a family member who can't stand your light, or that relentless inner critic whispering that you're too much, too fast, too bold. You know that feeling; the one that puts knots in your stomach and messes with your rhythm. You can feel the pull to shrink and to make yourself smaller just to keep the peace.

I've been there too. But the truth is, no matter how hard you try, you can't flip someone else's switch. That's their work to do, not yours. You can't rewrite their story, and you can't heal what they refuse to see. But you always have the power to flip your *own* switch.

GEM: You may not be able to control the interference, but you can always control your intention.

I've been there, idling too long when I could've been dancing to Bon Jovi's "It's My Life," but instead, I was frozen by the deafening silence of my passions, missing out on opportunities. Instead of owning my playbook, I let others try to rewrite it for me. I played it safe.

Flipping your switch through interference means protecting your peace while standing in your truth. It's about responding instead of reacting and being able to frame (and reframe) the noise around you instead of absorbing it.

When any form of interference shows up, it's your signal to adjust your own version of the un-piss yourself switch. Just remember, always pause first and end with movement.

— **Pause.** Reclaim your focus. Don't forget to breathe!

— **Rebalance your energy.** Shift your state. Get moving, get dancing, get your mojo back.

— **Reframe your story.** This is a great time to call on your inner cabinet!

— **Rewrite the next move of your playbook.** Always get yourself moving forward. Stay positively directed.

When you do this, the interference loses its grip. You move from "why me" to "watch me!" And here's where your inner cabinet earns its place. They're the ones who help you remember the truth when interference messes with your frequency. They see what's real when the noise gets loud, and they help you posture and offer strategy instead of defaulting to sympathy.

Cabinet Protocol

- Identify the interference. Name it clearly.

- Phone a cabinet member. Not to vent, but to ground you.

- Ask: What part of this is mine to own?

- Flip your perspective. Go from reaction to redirection.

The goal is to move forward with intention instead of acting on impulse.

GEM: What you do with what you know will define your leadership (and your legacy).

From Chaos to Clarity: Flip the Switch

The sleepless nights, the heartbreak, the chaos; I've stood in the middle of it, nearly broken, and realized that regardless of whether someone stays or leaves their company, family, or friends' circle, they sometimes also leave their energy. Meaning, they become a shell of themselves, like a house with the lights left on while no one is home. That was the moment I understood what it really means to flip the switch. We can't just turn the light on once and hope it stays lit. You must learn to find your power in the dark, over and over, until it becomes second nature.

The 6Ps became the scaffolding that rebuilt my life, leadership, and confidence. These are the tools that carried me from "I can't do this" to "I must do this" to "I'm already doing it." They've become the system I return to every time life shakes the ground under me.

You've learned the art. Now let's build the muscle. The 6Ps are the system that keeps your switch on, no matter what life throws your way.

Part 2: The Method that Powers the Flip

The 6Ps That Transform Everything

Flipping the switch is a practice, a mindset, and a way of being that turns a moment of fortitude into movement. It's not a motivational slogan or a quick fix but the muscle memory of courage and the discipline of self-leadership. It's the framework that'll help you rise every time you stumble. It's that split-second moment when something inside you says, *enough*. Enough waiting. Enough shrinking. Enough surviving on autopilot. It's the decision to flip the damn switch and step into the power that's been burning inside you all along.

And when you activate this model, the 6Ps rewire your entire system for purpose and forward motion. It's about programming yourself to find your power in the dark until it becomes second nature.

GEM: You're standing at the brink of transformation, and the only thing between you and your future self is the decision to flip the switch.

Like turning on a light, one shift can transform everything

✸ P1: Person - Elevate Your Mind, Body, and Spirit

Align your engine before you hit the gas.

Before you build anything extraordinary—career, family, goals, relationships—you have to elevate *you*. Not the auto-pilot version, but the *real* you. The one that's aligned, empowered, and ready to own your next chapter with conviction.

Your Person is your being, the sum of your mind, body, and spirit. Your being is the engine behind every big move you'll make. And when these three align, your power becomes unstoppable.

Your MIND: Master the inner game. It's time to rewrite the stories that keep you playing it safe. What are you feeding your mind today, fear or focus?

Grab that limiting belief, stare it down, and rewrite the damn thing! This takes practice, but the more you rewrite these limiting beliefs by flipping the switch, the more your subconscious mind will naturally begin doing this for you. You won't be waiting for permission anymore. You'll lead with intention, purpose, authenticity, and truth.

GEM: The moment you flip from "I can't" to "I can; therefore, I must," your entire system follows.

Your BODY: Treat it like the sacred vessel that carries your mission; every meeting, every experience, and every moment that matters to you. What would it look like to treat your body like your business depends on it (because it does)? But remember to keep it balanced.

Rest like a professional. Don't just sleep. *Rest.* You need real recovery. Listen to your body. Move with purpose and fuel wisely.

Your SPIRIT: Feed what lights you up. Hustle without soul burns you out, and fast. When was the last time you felt fully alive? And what were you doing?

I've loved what I do for most of my career, but it took me years to figure out why everyone else didn't feel the same. While coaching people early on, I kept digging into their deepest thoughts to uncover why they were so unsettled and unmotivated, when on the surface, it looked like they had it all together. Finally, I figured it out.

They didn't know how to feed their own soul.

Since before I can remember, I've fed my spirit because that's where joy lives. And joy has always been one of my core values. By feeding my spirit, the hustle became part of the excitement instead of contributing to the drain.

When your spirit is aligned with your truth, you walk differently. You speak differently. You lead differently. You move through the world like someone who knows exactly who they are and where they're headed. And that's even sexier than just being messy.

Elevate your Person: The Mirror Before the Move

- Mindset: Rewrite the limiting belief.

- Body: Move energy through movement.

- Spirit: Protect your joy rituals.

Inner Cabinet Cue: If in doubt, ask your truth-tellers how they see you showing up.

When your person is aligned (mind, body, and spirit), the next step is to give that alignment meaning. That's where Purpose enters.

✳ P2: Purpose - Know Your Why

Clarity is power and purpose is your battery.

Once you elevated who you are, the next step is knowing why you're here. Your "'why" isn't a luxury. It's not optional. It's your compass and your fuel to live the life you're truly meant to live! Purpose isn't something you find; it's remembered. It lives within your values, beliefs, and heartbreaks and in every experience that makes you who you are.

Ask yourself: What impact do I want to make today? And why does it matter so much to me? What values will I refuse to negotiate again? What would I still do even if no one noticed?

Purpose isn't something you stumble upon one day in Bali after a week of yoga and silence. I used to think that too; reading *Eat, Pray, Love* (Gilbert 2006) and believing maybe I needed to disappear somewhere exotic to find myself. But your Purpose isn't waiting for you in another place. It's already inside you. The space you need to find is in your heart and your mind, not on a map.

When you're clear on your Purpose, you stop chasing other people's definitions of success. You stop living with vague ambition. You start asking better questions, listening for the quiet wisdom of your own soul, and aligning your goals, your calendar, and your conversations with what actually matters.

You don't need to have it all figured out right now. You just need to begin. Because when you connect to your Purpose, everything sharpens, from your focus to your boundaries and even your courage.

This is your life. This is your legacy. The page is blank, and your Purpose is your pen. Don't hand it to someone else; you must write your own story.

Purpose Filter

- Does it align with my why?

- Does it drain or sustain me?

- Does it move me closer to my North Star?

Whatever you're focused on today, run it through these questions to ensure your actions are aligned with your Purpose.

GEM: When your "why" is clear, your how becomes instinct.

Purpose marks your "no" as being just as powerful as your "yes." And when your Purpose is clear, Passion finally has somewhere to go.

✴ P3: Passion - Ignite Your fire

Let your excitement lead the way.

Once you know why you're here, Passion decides how you show up. Protect your spark; it's your natural amplifier—no caffeine or extra vitamin B required. If Purpose is your "why," Passion is your hell yes! It's your ignition switch.

Red is the colour of Passion. It sounds romantic, sure. But Passion is fuel. It's fire. It's your lifeline back to what makes you feel alive. Jeffrey Gitomer nails it in his *Little Red Book of Selling*, "If you're not on fire, you will lose to someone who is" (Gitomer 2023). That's Passion.

Your time's finite, so flip the switch on it. You don't need more hours in a day. You just need more life in your hours. Reconnect to what lights you up! Make time for it, guard it fiercely, and let the excitement lead the way!

Ask yourself:

— When do I lose track of time (in the best possible way)?

— What would I run toward, not just show up for?

— What makes me smile before I even start doing it?

GEM: Passion is alignment in motion.

Passion is energy, but without direction, it becomes chaos. That's where your Playbook comes in.

✳ P4: Playbook - Design Your Roadmap

Strategy without a 'Today Step' is just a wish.

Passion gives you energy. The Playbook gives you direction. And having a strategy is what gives you freedom.

Your playbook isn't a list of goals but your personal roadmap between who you are now and who you're becoming. It's a living strategy that moves you instead of sitting on a shelf collecting dust or getting lost in the cloud. It's where you move from wishing to winning.

Future Self Planning

- North Star: The long game dream.

- 90 Day Bets: The big moves within reach.

- 7 Day Moves: What you'll execute this week.

- Today Step: The one thing you'll do now.

Inner Cabinet Cue: Share your Today Step with someone in your inner cabinet. Accountability keeps your momentum alive.

When I set my North Star, I wanted to become a CEO in an organization where people mattered, where leadership had meaning, and where both people and business could thrive. If I'd locked myself into one rigid path by telling myself it had to happen in one industry and in one way, I would've missed the opportunity to flip the switch from insurance to logistics, and this book might never have come to life.

Let your process evolve with you. Trust your vision, but don't marry the route. Let the Playbook shift. Because the path to your North Star might not look the way you imagined. You can truly only imagine what you know, what's hidden in your subconscious. So let go of control and let your Playbook lead you exactly where you're meant to go.

Instead of obsessing over the perfect plan (as you're probably doing right now), commit to consistent momentum. Forget chasing the formulas your parents, spouse, your friends handed you. That's someone else's formula. If you truly want to flip the switch, you must do this work on your own, when no one's watching. Let your life to this point be the proof and foundation for putting your name to your Playbook. Then move with it.

Once your dreams have a strategy, they're no longer "out there." They're already on their way. This is how leaders are built, through one clear, conscious decision at a time. Let your Playbook be the evidence of your vision. It'll remind you what you're made of and where you're going.

But even the best plan means nothing without endurance. And that's where Perseverance takes over.

✳ P5: Perseverance - Build Your Mental Toughness

Every dream worth chasing will test you—hard.

Even the best plan won't save you if you don't have the stamina to keep showing up for it. Perseverance isn't about force but about flow. It's choosing, repeatedly, not to be done yet. It's the fortitude without losing yourself in the process. It's the bravery to get back up, the courage to try again, and the wisdom to find the lesson in every setback.

Let that fuel you now. And remember, you're stronger than you think and far more capable than you give yourself credit for.

Persistence isn't a solo sport. It's about showing up vulnerable and reaching out to your inner cabinet when others retreat. It's about choosing not to give up even when the wins take longer than expected. Sometimes the most powerful move is showing up while everyone else sits it out.

When it gets hard, ask yourself:

— Does this still serve my why?

— Does this light my fire or dim it?

— Does this bring me closer to my North Star?

Hard Pause Check-in

- Am I forcing or flowing?

- Is this challenge building or breaking me?

- What's one small win I can own today?

GEM: Perseverance stops being a struggle when your purpose is solid.

Because even grit needs community. That's where Partnership changes everything.

✳ P6: Partnership - Your Inner Cabinet

Your Inner Cabinet is your expansion strategy.

Even the strongest grit needs good company. Because no matter how self driven you are, you're not meant to do this alone. You can go fast alone, but we'll always go *farther* together. At some point, you'll need someone to remind you of who you are; someone to offer a hand, a new perspective, a nudge, or even just a safe space to say, *"I'm tired, but I'm still in it."*

You weren't put on this earth to be alone. Your dreams are too big, your impact is too powerful, and your unique and brilliant way about you is too bright to keep it all to yourself.

This is your opportunity to be challenged, celebrated, and stretched in ways you simply can't do in isolation. The right people by your side (whether they're your mentors, teammates, loved ones, or fellow dreamers) will remind you of your purpose when doubt creeps in and will push you to keep flipping the switch when you're tempted to turn the lights out.

Trust Check for Inner Cabinet (HERS)

- **Honesty:** Do they tell me the truth even when it's hard?

- **Empathy:** Do they see my humanity before my title?

- **Reliability:** Do they always follow through when it matters?

- **Skill:** Do they stretch my thinking and fuel my growth?

GEM: Leadership isn't a solo sport. Partnership is your power source.

The Courage Trifecta: Divorce, Relocation, Reinvention

2007 was the year I stopped waiting for permission to live my life. I stood at a crossroads, with my marriage ending, motherhood beginning, and career shifting, all colliding into one unplanned season that demanded courage I didn't know I had. The reflection in the mirror was a woman I no longer recognized. I was exhausted. I felt disconnected on so many levels and as if I were running on autopilot 24/7. I was done.

Then came Lexi, one small human who lit up everything I'd buried. Her arrival the previous year forced me to look at what I'd been tolerating. I couldn't hide behind safety anymore. I wanted her to see a woman who stood for her truth, even when it cost her comfort. Flipping the switch meant I had to stop surviving and actively rewrite my story while seemingly *no one was watching*. I didn't have a plan, but I had a decision.

That February, with shaking hands and a heart that felt heavier than a ton of bricks, I said the words out loud: "I'm leaving." It wasn't rebellion but the quiet knowing that I could no longer live small and still call it love.

I moved back to my hometown to come home to myself. My nana's words echoed in my head. "Financial security isn't about wealth. It's about choice." I bought a small house in my own name, and when the keys dropped into my hand, I'd just signed my declaration of independence. I wasn't waiting to be rescued; I was saving myself.

When it came to my career, leaving the partnership in a firm I helped shape wasn't just a career move but a deliberate act of courage. It was brutal, but it was also necessary. It wasn't about chasing a title anymore. It hadn't been for a long time. Instead, it was about building a life that aligned with my truth, and stepping into a new role in sales leadership closer to home was the start of how I would accomplish that. It gave me proximity to my daughter, my roots, and my future.

I called that year my "Courage Trifecta." Divorce, relocation, and reinvention. Three hard resets that demanded every ounce of perseverance and faith.

On nights when the weight of it all nearly crushed me, I'd call my nana for wine or my godmother for prayer, depending on what kind of night it was. My inner cabinet was small, but it was mighty. They didn't fix my problems for me. How could they? Nor did they just cheer by the sideline. They stood as witnesses to my rebuilding and helped me walk through fire so I could rise stronger. They reminded me that sometimes courage looks like holding steady when everything feels uncertain.

GEM: Every time you choose action over fear, the world moves to meet you.

Fast forward twenty years; what once felt like the end of everything was the beginning of *me*. That year stripped me bare, but it also built the foundation I stand on today. It taught me that security is about freedom, not money or accolades. It taught me that endings are just disguised new beginnings. And it taught me that playing it safe is the fastest way to lose yourself.

When I stopped fearing failure and started fearing regret, that's when everything changed. I started designing my life instead of defending it. My playbook evolved with me—flexible, messy, honest—led intentionally by the woman I was becoming. My future self became my compass, and every decision (including every risk) was filtered through her lens.

I would ask myself, "What would she want from me right now?" The answer was always some version of courage. So, I listened.

GEM: Dreams expand to the size of your decisions.

Every brave choice stretched the boundaries of what I believed was possible. And that's what flipping the switch is really about! Not *changing* who you are but remembering *who* you truly are. It's about stepping into your full power and living like you were never meant to play small. Because you weren't. None of us were. And we need to stop allowing the world to make us believe otherwise.

I flipped the switch, but it took all of the 6Ps to do it. That's how I developed a life I could see and feel in full color. Each P lit up a new path forward, shaping a life built on intention, anchored in purpose, and open to incredible possibility.

Maybe you're asking yourself, *do I really need all six?* I get it. It's tempting to skip one, to lean on your strengths and sidestep what feels harder. But every P is a strand of your power, and when one's missing, the current doesn't flow. When you commit to all six, the light stays on instead of endlessly flickering. Effortlessly and continuously, you become the source of your own illumination, and your future self finally walks into the room, already home.

The Hardest P to Flip

Without a doubt, the hardest P to flip is Person, elevating your mind, body, and spirit. Because before you can build anything lasting, you must face the truth about yourself and focus on elevation.

It's the part most people rush past. They jump straight to the strategy, and the to-do lists because it's easier to rearrange your schedule than to rewrite your story. But none of the tangible moves you make hold any weight if the person behind it isn't elevated and aligned. You can't outsource *becoming*.

That's why I had to start by flipping the switch on **my own story**. I wasn't starting from scratch, but I was starting from stuck. Stuck in a narrative that was shaped by fear, tradition, and the heavy weight of other people's expectations. I knew what needed to be done, but first, I had to face *who I was being*.

I had to face my own conditioning and the voices that said, "What will people think?" Will they still be proud of me?" The same guilt and fear of being seen as a woman who walked away. But I wasn't walking away from anything. I was walking toward my truth, toward a version of me who was ready to lead from authenticity instead of giving into the expectations of others.

P1 Insight: Elevate Your Person

- Reframe: I'm not leaving. I am realigning.

- Reminder: Fear is often the price of freedom.

- Reflection: Who am I becoming when I stop negotiating with my truth?

Once I reclaimed my own story, everything else began to line up: my purpose sharpened, my passion returned, and my partnerships deepened. My Playbook finally reflected me. And I named my Playbook, *My Future Self Takes the Lead.*

So here we are—you and me—at the threshold of your own flip. You've seen how the light shifts when you choose courage, how the noise fades when you lead with intention, and how the switch doesn't stay on because of luck but because you do the work.

This is your invitation to stop shrinking and start shining. To step into your next chapter instead of waiting for validation, guided by your own inner power. To build your life, your leadership, and your legacy with the same conviction you once reserved for everyone else. This is your time.

GEM: The flip isn't louder; it's truer.

Flip the switch. Focus on living a life that's aligned with your voice and values. When you actually do this, the world will rearrange itself around your honesty. That's where change becomes real, where you stop playing it safe and start living wide awake.

Your Pocket Flip-Kit: 3 Key Takeaways

1. The flip starts in private

Do the work when no one is watching. Lead from raw self awareness instead of performance and borrow the eyes of your inner cabinet when your own vision blurs.

2. All 6Ps or it stalls

Person, Purpose, Passion, Playbook, Perseverance, Partnership; each is a strand of your power. Leave one out and the current doesn't flow. Start with Person and let Partnership (your inner cabinet) keep the lights on.

3. Interference + Pause + Today Step

You can't control other people's switch, only yours. Breathe, rebalance, and reframe. Call your Cabinet, then take the Today Step your future self would ask for. Decisions create momentum, and momentum creates change.

Flip the Switch Moment

Who's really sitting at your metaphorical kitchen table, the place where truth is spoken, courage is built, and hard conversations are welcome? And perhaps even more importantly, who's missing that deserves a seat?

Your inner cabinet is the circle that keeps your light on, the people who challenge you, champion you, and keep you grounded when the world gets noisy. Think quality over quantity and intention over proximity.

Fuel for the Fire

— **Visionaries:** Expand your thinking; remind yourself to dream boldly.

— **Mentors:** Share wisdom from the roads you're walking now.

— **Supporters:** Offer belief and love on the days you doubt yourself.

— **Critics (with care):** Speak the truth with respect and stretch your blind spots.

— **Collaborators:** Turn ideas into movement.

— **Connectors:** Open doors and link you to new possibilities.

— **Experts:** Lend specialized insight when stakes are high.

1. **Name them.** Write down the names of those who currently fill each seat. Leave blanks where you have gaps.

2. **Evaluate.** Who fuels you? Who drains you? Who needs a bigger role or less of one? Write them down.

3. **Balance.** Aim for 8–12 trusted voices with depth, diversity, and soul alignment.

4. **Activate.** Reach out to one person this week, to strengthen or bond or invite a new voice to the table.

ACTIVATE NOW!
Sample Outreach to Activate Your Inner Cabinet:

To: Prospective Cabinet Member

Subject: An Invitation to Join My Inner Cabinet

Dear _______. I'm curating a small inner cabinet—trusted voices who challenge me, ground me, and help me lead with purpose, clarity and courage. You're someone whose perspective I deeply value because _______, and I would be honoured to explore whether this season is the right moment for us to support each other with more intention.

Would you be open to a 20-minute call next week? I'll come prepared with one clear ask—and one meaningful way I can add value in return.

Block the call. Put it in the calendar. Momentum is a promise you keep to your future self.

CHAPTER 3

Keep it R.E.A.L.

*"My friends, all I'm trying to say is that if we are to
go forward today, we've got to go back
and rediscover some mighty precious values
that we've left behind."*
— Martin Luther King Jr.

GEM: *When you read the past with honesty, you wire the future with purpose.*

The first time I realized how powerful R.E.A.L. leadership was, it happened in a moment of silence. I'd just finished delivering some tough news to my team about a change no one wanted. I looked up, ready for resistance, but instead, people leaned in. It wasn't a result of blind agreement or some form of giving in, but a sign that they trusted how I said it.

Leadership isn't about having all the right words. It's about being real enough with what you do say, that people still feel safe when everything else feels uncertain.

If some of what we've learned in the last two chapters still feels unsettling—if you're wrestling with a decision, or your gut is saying something has to change—that's why we are here, walking through this together. You're learning to flip the switch so the life you want, becomes the life you live.

Now, let's take that same energy and apply it to how you lead. Because once you've flipped the switch within yourself, the next challenge is keeping it on when the world tests your integrity. That's what R.E.A.L. leadership is all about, rediscovering those precious values that too many leaders have traded for image, speed, or control.

Leadership used to mean power, control, and perfection. But real leadership, the kind that builds trust and momentum, looks different. It's raw, it's honest, and deeply human. It's R.E.A.L.

Somewhere along the climb between ambition, exhaustion, and expectation, many leaders traded real for right. But right doesn't inspire trust. So how do we lead in a way that's real, grounded, and human when the world moves faster than our breath?

Keep it R.E.A.L.

R Resilience: Stay steady when storms hit.

E Empathy: Lead with understanding instead of assumption.

A Authenticity: Show up as the same person in every room.

L Legacy: Live and lead in a way that leaves others stronger than you found them.

R.E.A.L. leadership isn't a performance but who you become when you align your actions with your values. And it's powered by the 6Ps.

— **R**esilience is powered by your **Perseverance.**

— **E**mpathy is powered by your **Partnership** with your inner cabinet.

— **A**uthenticity is powered by your **Person** and **Passion.**

— **L**egacy is powered through your **Purpose** and your **Playbook.**

It all comes full circle.

Leadership isn't about perfection, it's about being R.E.A.L.

R - Resilience: The Rep After the Miss

One afternoon at Lexi's basketball game, she missed a key free throw. The defeat hit her face and body: the slumped shoulders, the trembling lip. My instinct screamed, *Run to her. Fix it.* But Stephene caught my hand. "Wait."

We did. We watched as she took a deep breath, reset her stance, and stepped back to the line. *Swish.* The sound of the ball hitting the net was everything. But it wasn't the point that mattered. What mattered was watching her rise after missing.

Motherhood's been my greatest leadership classroom. As a single mom, I spent years questioning myself. *Am I doing this right? Are the choices I'm making, the words I'm speaking, shaping Lexi into the best version of herself?* In those early years, clouded by divorce, a difficult custody battle, and pure exhaustion, I was my own toughest critic. I replayed my mistakes on a loop, convinced that every miss meant failure. And I was too busy criticizing myself to celebrate the courage it took to take the shot in the first place.

Then came Stephene, who entered our lives with steadiness and grace. He hadn't parented before, so his playbook was "figure it out as you go," just like mine! But watching him step into the role of an engaged stepdad for Lexi—whether it was teaching her how to make her own lunch at age six, showing her complex mathematical equations by age eight, or encouraging her to push through teenage doubts—uncovered some core truths about life. His calm presence shifted the energy in our home. "Just wait, Dianna," he'd say gently. "She's got this." And somehow, I believed him. Because he was right every time.

That moment on the court still reminds me that what matters is the repetition after the miss. Every miss carries a message you can only hear if you stay on the court. And when you've stayed in the court long enough, you realize perseverance isn't a solo act.

Reflection: What's the next shot you've been avoiding? Name the smallest repetition you can take today.

E - Empathy: Compassion that Raises the Bar

During the pandemic, uncertainty became our new normal and the old playbooks were useless, but our company president led with radical transparency. At our first virtual town hall, he said, "I don't know exactly how this will turn out, but I promise, we'll face it together." That moment of honesty steadied a company full of anxious hearts.

Instead of layoffs, he developed a three-week work cycle followed by a one-week furlough for every person, including him. When the rebound came, he said, "We'll all end the year whole." And he kept that promise; every furlough week was paid back.

Empathy told the truth. Accountability shared the load. Trust did the math. That's how a R.E.A.L. culture compounds. Empathy and trust are the true currency of leadership (and of our humanity) that deepen accountability. The best leaders don't let people off the hook but instead walk beside them as they climb together.

When we listen deeply and seek to truly understand, we build bridges. Empathy is the lifeline of trust, and trust is the foundation of everything. It starts within, trusting our own abilities fuels confidence. Extending the same to others creates an environment of respect and authenticity that changes everything.

R.E.A.L leadership isn't about walking into a room with all the answers. Because none of us can claim to have all the answers. It's about walking in as you are (warts, worries, and all) and choosing to lead anyway. When leaders prioritize empathy, they unlock a team that's strong, loyal, and ready to weather any storm together.

Reflection: What truth needs saying, and how can you say it with care? Where can you set one clearer expectation this week?

A - Authenticity: Presence Over Polish

It was Lexi's junior kindergarten bake sale. The gym smelled like sugar and echoed the sweet sounds of children ready to indulge themselves. Tables overflowed with Pinterest-perfect desserts while I stood there in a suit and heels, holding a plastic container of store-bought cupcakes.

Lexi squeezed my hand, eyes wide and trusting. "Mom", she whispered, "they're still cupcakes."

I laughed. "You're right. Let's bring some commercial flair to this bake sale!"

We placed our cupcakes beside a tower of homemade brownies. And within minutes, kids were grabbing ours first. One little boy yelled, "These are my favourite!" Lexi's face glowed.

Later, a mom leaned over and said, "I was up until midnight baking. I wish I'd done what you did."

We laughed. We were two very different people, two very different kinds of mothers, and yet, we were still "the same" in that moment. Perfection is overrated (and completely unattainable). Presence is everything. That moment reminded me that being real, especially when you feel out of place, is the ultimate act of confidence.

Chasing perfection is the enemy of connection. Authenticity doesn't ask you to shine, but rather, it asks you to *show up*. Let go of the pressure to have it all figured out. Let your flaws, cracks, and messy moments out, because they're what make you real and memorable. They make you *you*.

GEM: Your cracks aren't weakness. They're how your light gets in when your truth gets out.

Reflection: What filter can you drop today? Where are you mistaking polish for presence?

L - Legacy: What You Carry, Not How It Shines

I travel a lot, and I often think of my legacy like my favourite carry-on. It sounds weird but hear me out. My carry-on is scuffed, but it's reliable. Every mark on it tells a story of risks I've taken, lessons I've learned, and the imprints left on the hearts and minds of people I loved along the way (all adding pages to my playbook). That's what legacy is; not how it looks, but what it holds.

Legacy once felt like a burden, something heavy I had to live up to. But over time, I realized legacy is more about motion and movement than building some kind of monument. It's what you carry forward, not what you leave behind.

Every day you're packing something new—kindness, courage, wisdom, truth, and so many wins, lessons, and intimate experiences. Make sure what you carry reflects who you're becoming. Living your legacy is being completely okay with who you are in the dark of night, so that in the light of day, you're beyond "okay" with who you're becoming.

Reflection: If your carry-on could talk, what story would it tell about this season of your playbook? What are you packing on purpose, and what needs to be left out?

Keeping it R.E.A.L. at Home (Why it Matters Everywhere)

R.E.A.L. leadership doesn't stop when you log off or leave the office. The same truths that build trust in teams also hold families together. Keeping it R.E.A.L. has been my anchor personally, professionally and in every relationship I care about. It's been both my guide and my practice, and one of the most rewarding commitments I've ever made that powers my ability to flip the switch.

For years, I didn't realize that my personal playbook (as a mom, as a wife, a professional woman and a leader in male-dominated spaces) had been in draft mode. So, when that truth finally hit me, it felt like uncovering buried treasure. A true "aha" moment. I could see that every success, every setback, and every twist in my journey had been quietly shaping a playbook that was 100% mine. I owned it. It was built from my wins, my lessons, and my lived experience. And that discovery changed everything.

Fast forward to today: Lexi is a young woman, full of life, ambition, and clearly rooted in her potential as she heads into her second year of university. She's bold, curious, and unapologetically herself. Yet, dropping her off that first year was harder than many challenges I've faced. It should have been part of my playbook, but that emotion threw me for a loop. The drive home was quiet. The house was even quieter. And for days, I'd pause when I walked by her empty room, the ache of both loss and pride in my gut. The silence had a weight, but it also had possibility. And for the first time in years, I could hear my own heartbeat again.

That's the thing about change. It carries two stories: one ending, and one beginning. The work is learning to hold both, and for me, the drop off was signalling the end of her childhood but also the beginning of a remarkable chapter of possibility in her playbook, as well as mine.

The bond Lexi and I share today is stronger than ever because it's built on honesty. We love fiercely, argue boldly, and laugh until we cry. Shopping together is our favourite chaos because we're the same clothing size, same shoe size, and have a similar style. Which means constant stealing and playful back and forth with laughter that fills the house.

When things get tense, which often happens with two fiercely passionate women, Stephene steps in with his calm grin. "What would your future selves say right now about this?" That question brings us back to center. But it's that fire, that messy realness, that keeps us so tight. We laugh, we clash, we steal each other's clothes, and somehow, we always end up closer because of it.

As a parent, you never know if you've raised your child or just survived them until you see them thriving on their own. And a bonus is when they still want you in their world for all R.E.A.L. and messy moments. Lexi's authenticity burns so bright, too bright sometimes, that I often go looking for my shades to shield me from what's coming next. She tells me things I would rather not know, but I wouldn't trade it for anything. Her unfiltered honesty means trust runs both ways.

And that's the deal, right? I raised her to be unapologetically herself, authentically imperfect. That's what keeping it R.E.A.L. really means: building connections that can hold the truth.

This journey of embracing our truths as a family has helped us draft our own paths that form beautifully together. We have individual playbooks, all living in harmony with one another, creating a legacy for each of us that's rooted in keeping it R.E.A.L. as one family unit.

The Flip from Authenticity to Assertion

When you choose to keep it R.E.A.L., you're choosing to live in it. It's how you show up when no one is watching; how you listen when silence feels safer and how you tell the truth when your voice shakes.

R.E.A.L. leaders don't chase validation but instead create transformation. They don't wear masks to fit the room. They bring the room back to the truth, even when it's not always comfortable.

Authenticity will test your courage. Empathy will stretch your patience. Perseverance will demand full recovery. And legacy will ask you to stay the course when the applause fades. This is what truly separates managers from leaders, and leaders from legends. Being R.E.A.L. is how trust is earned and how your future self will recognize you when you get there.

GEM: When you stay R.E.A.L., you choose leadership over performance.

Your Pocket Flip-Kit: 3 Key Takeaways

1. Lead from the inside out

Flip the switch within yourself before you try to light the room. When you lead from alignment rather than approval, people feel it, and energy is contagious. Make yours trustworthy.

2. Replace performance with presence

You don't have to have the perfect words, plan, or posture. What people want is your truth, not some form of unrealistic polish. Drop the mask, take a breath, and lead with your whole self, cracks, courage, and all.

3. Build legacy in motion

Legacy isn't something you leave behind but something you carry forward every day. The small repetitions of fortitude, empathy, authenticity, and integrity are what compound into the trust that outlasts you.

- **R**esilience is built on the repetition after the miss.

- **E**mpathy tells the truth and shares the load.

- **A**uthenticity trades polish for presence.

- **L**egacy carries forward what matters most.

Flip the Switch Moment:

Now it's your time to get R.E.A.L.! Grab a cozy spot, pour yourself a favorite cup of joy, and open your journal.

Spark Questions:

R - Resilience:

— What next shot am I avoiding? What's the smallest rep I can take today?

— What from my past playbook proves I can do hard things?

E - Empathy + Trust:

— What truth needs saying, and how will I say it with care?

— Where can I set one clearer expectation this week?

A - Authenticity:

— What filter can I drop today?

— Where am I mistaking polish for presence?

L - Legacy:

— If my carry-on could talk, what story would it tell me about this season of my playbook?

— What am I packing on purpose, and what needs to be left out?

Inner Cabinet Cue: Who steadies me? Who stretches me? Who tells me the truth?

Leading with authenticity takes guts! And grace. Fail forward. Lead with empathy. Speak the truth. Show up fully in your light and in your cracks.

Pick one R.E.A.L. move in the next 24 hours. Make the call. Tell the truth. Take the next shot. That's how you flip the switch, again and again, until the light feels natural.

Author's Note:

The Beauty in the Messy Middle

Life will never ask you to be perfect, but it will keep inviting you to be present.

The real growth happens in the moments you would rather skip; the missed shots, the messy middles, and the awkward pauses that make you face yourself. That's where courage shows up, and let's be honest, it's hard and uncomfortable.

But when you stop cleaning up your edges and start owning them, something powerful happens. When people actually see how you wear your edges, they lean in closer. They start to see themselves in your story, and that's where trust begins and connection deepens.

So, if things feel chaotic right now, take a breath. You aren't breaking; you're becoming. The cracks, the chaos, and the real-life swirl of it all is where the magic hides.

Being messy isn't the detour but the path in disguise. It's the proof that you're alive, learning, and flipping the switch. You're leading from a place that is 100% real, and that's what truly makes it sexy.

Stay Inspired,

CHAPTER 4

Excuse Me! You're in My Way

"You miss one hundred percent
of the shots you don't take."
— *Wayne Gretzky*

The first time I said it out loud, my voice trembled because for years, I'd trained myself to stay polite when I was angry, agreeable when I was exhausted, and quiet when I knew I was right.

I looked across the table and said, as calmly as I could, "Excuse me. You're in my way." It wasn't harsh or dramatic. It was just the truth, and one I'd swallowed a hundred times before, until I finally couldn't anymore.

That moment changed something in me. I realized that speaking up wasn't inherently going to lead to confrontation and that saying what needed to be said was about honouring myself. Looking back, it wasn't about the other person. It was about me reclaiming the space

I'd been slowly giving away through over-explaining, over-pleasing and over-performing.

You need to learn to stand in your space, even when it feels uncomfortable. Because when you start showing up taller, as your full self, not everyone will know what to do with your light. Some will pull back. Some will test you. But others, the people you actually want in your life, will quietly cheer from the sidelines.

The point isn't to be liked. The point is to be *you*.

You've done the work. You have started keeping it R.E.A.L. by being more transparent and honest in how you lead and live. But like any new relationship, you're still figuring it out. You're learning what fits, what stretches you, and (my personal favourite) what lights you up. But awareness can only take you so far. And at some point, you have to take the shot.

When Wayne Gretzky was asked what made him one of the greatest hockey players of all time, he said, "I skate to where the puck is going to be, not to where it has been." While everyone else chased the puck, Wayne moved toward possibility; he moved to what was next. He went where no one else went, and he scored, often.

That's the work we need to do, learning to have the courage to move toward what's next, even when no one else sees it yet.

GEM: Dare to be Different, not safe.

But the reality is, every time you step forward, something will try to block your path. An old fear, a noisy opinion, a system built for someone else's comfort. We can spend our whole lives reacting to what's already happened, explaining, defending, and catching up. Or we can move and make progress by skating toward the future we want to create. And the moment you stop waiting for permission and start trusting your own direction, you become unstoppable.

The hardest part about taking the shot isn't the miss but the moment before you move. It's the hesitation. The voice that says, "What if you're wrong?" or "What if they don't like it?" That's the same voice that used to stop me from speaking up at meetings, asking for what I needed, or applying for the role I knew I could do.

We all have the instinct to hesitate. It's a form of protection. But there comes a time when protecting your comfort starts charging a price you can't afford. And it always collects the same thing first: your confidence. Confidence is your quiet currency of progress, and when you start spending it on fear, it takes time to earn it back.

The antidote to fear has always been movement.

There's something powerful that happens when you finally move. You realize you're not fighting people anymore but outgrowing patterns. You stop trying to convince others you belong and start believing it yourself.

Taking your shot doesn't mean charging in like a bull without thought. It means trusting your preparation and having faith in your instincts and worth, especially when the outcome isn't guaranteed.

True courage isn't loud or flashy. It's often a quiet power, clear and honest. It sounds like, "This is my idea," or "That's not okay with me," or "I'm ready for more." And sometimes it sounds exactly like, "Excuse me. You're in my way."

Every time you choose to take the shot, you grow your leadership in ways a course or title never could. You start building internal muscles you never thought you had, the kind that strengthen with every difficult conversion, every boundary held, and every truth told.

The leaders I coach often ask, "How do I know when to speak up?" The answer is simply, when silence starts costing you more than honesty. Because silence has a price, and usually that price is higher than speaking up. It pays using your energy, your ideas, and your joy.

Think about the last time you held back in a meeting, a relationship, or even a personal decision that you may be contemplating right now. You've probably replayed it many times in your head, thinking of all the things you could've said. This is what happens when we let fear drive us.

Even if your voice shakes, say the thing. Even if it's awkward. Take a step. Courage lives in the messy middle between fear and action. Not every shot you take will go in, but every shot you don't take guarantees nothing changes. And you didn't come this far to stay the same.

Follower or R.E.A.L. Disruptor?

When you see those two choices, which one speaks to who you are? Follower or Disruptor? I don't mean the loud, self-serving kind of disruptor we see on social media, but the kind fueled by empathy, authenticity, and strength. The kind who leads change that matters.

Have you noticed yourself slipping back into playing it safe? You hold back your voice, you blend in, you stay in comfort when your gut is crying for courage?

I love working with leaders who want to change that. My favourite kind of work happens when we go deep, when we peel back everything that isn't real and get clear on what drives us (truth, purpose, and legacy). Because when leadership is built on those things, the disruption created is lasting and full of heart.

Whether you're leading a team, raising kids, mentoring others, or charting your own next move, your authenticity is your edge. What makes you *you* isn't a trait so much as a power source. It's what gives you the courage to move through uncertainty with understanding and confidence. That's where real growth and innovation live.

The Power of *What If:* Playing R.E.A.L.

After a big promotion, I was walking on cloud 9. I felt confident and excited about what was ahead. My boss (who'd guided me for years) was retiring, and I was ready to learn under new leadership. But not long after stepping into the role, feedback started coming my way from my new leader but also several of my male colleagues outside the country. During business interactions and board presentations, the phrase kept surfacing, "You need to block and tackle more, Dianna."

At first, I laughed it off. But it kept coming back. The same words. The same tone. It became less a suggestion and more an expectation I didn't understand.

While I can appreciate a good sports analogy, this one left me more unsettled than inspired. I couldn't help but wonder, *what great leader wakes up in the morning thinking about blocking and tackling?* Unless you're suiting up for battle, that mindset feels out of step and disconnected.

It was one of those moments in my career where I had to take a hard pause.

The Safe Moment

For a while, I almost gave in. When I first heard those words, something tightened inside me. My first thought was, *I can't*. Not because I didn't know how to lead, but because it went against everything I believed in. My leadership was built on connection. I led with trust instead of favouring tactics.

Still, underneath that conviction sat fear. What if this was the end? What if my leadership no longer fit? This company had become a part of me; the people who influenced my career and those I helped to build theirs. Walking away would mean leaving behind a part of myself.

The safe thing to do would've been to stay quiet, follow the rules, and keep the peace. But safety rarely leads to growth. So, I sat in the tension between who I was *expected* to be and who I knew I was. And that's when it hit me: this wasn't about them. It was about me. It was about my values, my integrity, and my future self watching to see what I'd do.

I had to flip the switch.

GEM: Stretch moments are soul moments. They test your edges and reveal your essence.

I went back to my personal playbook where those lessons lived that were written in sweat and late nights, replaying in my mind the small wins that mattered. I called on my inner cabinet, the trusted voices who reminded me of who I am. And through some raw, real conversations with my executive coach, I reignited my purpose, passion, understanding, and courage. It wasn't about surviving a boss but choosing the kind of leader I wanted to be and the kind of legacy I wanted to carry forward.

My leadership was different, but not because I was a woman. I just never fit the mold. I wasn't the one with every technical answer. I was the one who believed that people are the heartbeat of success. Business results soar when people feel trusted, seen, and inspired because they perform at their best. And that's always been my playbook. The challenge wasn't about skill but about difference. And that difference turned out to be my breakthrough.

So, I started asking myself:

— What if my way, my trust-driven, people-first way, was exactly what this organization needed?

— What if leading with empathy and authenticity could drive results and change the culture?

— What if this wasn't a wall but an opening?

The more I leaned into those questions, the clearer the answer became. One word and three letters full of possibility: yes.

GEM: By daring to ask, "What if?" We unlock the power to turn challenges into opportunities.

I decided to quietly disrupt the old playbook by replacing commands with curiosity and connection and rigidity with trust. And then one day, it happened. Our new CEO stood on stage at the global capital markets day event, and the first slide behind him had one word: Trust.

That word became our company's foundation, and that moment confirmed what I already knew. That I'd skated to where the puck was going, and we scored.

Over the next three years, everything changed. Gender parity on our executive team; national recognition as one of the Most Trusted Executive Teams; Great Place to Work certifications and badges earned, year after year; financial performance and market growth was strong. Flipping the switch in that moment sparked a company-wide movement built on R.E.A.L. leadership.

GEM: The most powerful disruption comes from authenticity; showing up as yourself, even when it's messy.

The Future Belongs to the Disruptors

Stepping into leadership is about standing out, not fitting in. R.E.A.L. leaders don't follow the playbooks of those who came before them;

they write their own. The future doesn't look like the past, nor should your leadership.

We need playbooks that evolve faster than technology, driven by human creativity, empathy, and conviction. R.E.A.L. leadership means leading with integrity and disrupting with heart. What once felt soft has become the strongest force of change.

The moment you start living from truth instead of approval, people will notice. Some will be inspired, and some will feel threatened. But both reactions are reflections of where *they* are, and where you've grown.

Your Pocket Flip-Kit: 3 Key Takeaways

1. Authenticity is your competitive advantage

The world doesn't need another copycat leader. Your authenticity is what sets you apart and gives you the courage to disrupt with heart. When you lead with empathy, honesty, and truth, you create the kind of impact that lasts.

2. "I can't" is your turning point, not your limit

That moment of hesitation—the one that makes you question yourself—is an act of wisdom asking you to realign. Listen to it, then flip the switch from "I can't" to "I must." That shift is where courage is born.

3. R.E.A.L. disruption starts from within

True disruption doesn't begin in boardrooms or strategies but in you. Every time you choose integrity over comfort, connection over control, and purpose over perfection, you become the kind of leader who changes the game.

Flip the Switch Moment

Grab your journal, and let's take some time to reflect on the ways in which you can positively disrupt the environment you are leading (whether it's at home, at school, in the office, or in your community). How can you focus more on where the puck is going?

Power Move: How to Craft your R.E.A.L. Disruption

You've had your own block-and-tackle moment in one version or another, the one that made you whisper, "Are you kidding me? I can't." Maybe it sounded like, "I can't speak up yet," or "I can't lead that way," or "I can't risk what I've built." That hesitation is the most vulnerable part of you speaking up. "I can't" isn't about capability but whether you're in alignment with who you really are. It's your inner compass saying something's off.

When that voice shows up, don't ignore it. Instead, pause. Listen to the message and get your body moving a little to shift the energy. Reframe, then flip it. Shift from "I can't" to "I must." Because what you must do is usually the one thing that moves you, and everyone watching you move forward.

GEM: "I can't" is often your soul whispering, "you must." Listen closely.

1. Where is the Puck Now, and Where Is It Heading?

Look around you. Where is everyone's attention right now, and where is your puck really going? Let your thoughts flow. The seventieth idea might be the one that changes everything. Then imagine your future self in that moment, the one who already knows where the puck is heading. What does she see that you don't yet?

2. Clear the Pathways for Innovation

Name what's in your way, externally and internally. Then turn those barriers into stepping stones. Reframe your thinking from "I can't" to "I must." Go back to your playbook and remember the moments that stretched you, the ones that proved your strength. Take the shot. Your perseverance needs the repetition.

3. Harness Your Superpower to Transform

What's your greatest strength, your superpower? That's the energy that fuels your growth and everyone else's. Use it to lead with empathy, build trust, and keep your focus on where the puck is going, not where it's been.

4. Celebrate and Amplify Your Differences

Think about what sets you apart. How does your authentic style challenge old patterns and redefine what leadership looks like where you are? Those differences are your runway.

5. Strategize Your Disruptive Path and Fuel Your Legacy

Ask yourself, "What do my people truly need right now? And how can my superpower help take them there?" Design a plan that puts your strengths and insights to work. Let it redefine how you lead and inspire the people around you to rise with you.

When you do this work, when you show up with courage and conviction, you move from participant to catalyst.

GEM: R.E.A.L. disruption is courage rooted in truth, powered by empathy, and delivered with purpose.

Flipping the switch isn't a single moment but a way of being. The world is waiting for your light. Will you stay where it's safe, or will you skate toward what's next and crush it? Trust yourself. Flip the switch. Be a R.E.A.L. Disruptor.

Author's Note:

Say it Anyway

I still get nervous when I speak up in high pressure situations. My voice still shakes sometimes. And although it's crazy uncomfortable, I'm okay with that, because silence used to cost me more than a shaky voice ever will.

You won't always say it perfectly. You might draw a line and second-guess it later, and that's okay. Every time you use your voice with honesty and care, you build trust with yourself. And the more you trust yourself, the less approval you need from anyone else.

So, if your voice trembles, let it. It just means you're finally using it.

Stay Inspired,

CHAPTER 5

From Envy to Empowerment

*"A great pleasure in life is doing
what people say you cannot do."*
— *Walter Bagehot*

GEM: Let their limits light your fuse.

You did it! You found your voice. Maybe it still shakes sometimes, but the truth doesn't need to be loud to be powerful.

Now comes what happens when that voice starts to draw attention, and not all of it is kind. That's where envy enters. Yours, theirs, the world's. It's time to flip it, turning comparison and criticism into pure empowerment. Because every time you rise above someone's limitation, you reset what's possible for you and for them.

You've seen how authenticity fuels R.E.A.L. leadership and transforms you into a R.E.A.L. Disruptor. You've stepped into courage, taken your shot, and claimed your space. Now, as you keep rising, speed bumps appear; eye rolls, silence arrives, subtle digs slip out, or that comparison trap creeps in. And that pull you feel is envy. Sometimes theirs, but sometimes yours. This is where we flip the switch to stop letting it drain and start using it to drive us.

Envy has two faces. Theirs shows up as subtle digs or silence when you rise. Our own creeps in when you scroll through someone else's highlight reel and start questioning your own pace. Both are teachers but in different ways. One asks for boundaries, and the other asks for self-investment.

Pink Gloves and Pimples

Early in my executive career, the president asked me to present a new risk product to our National Management Board. Two women (including me) out of fifteen in the room, and my division was the underdog.

I prepped like a fighter, preparing a story more than spreadsheets. Insurance isn't usually exciting, but this product had the potential to change the game, so I had to lean in and make the complex seem simple. The story linked risk, protection, and profit to what actually mattered to them, and our conversion rates were the highest in the company—I was proud.

But halfway through my presentation, the president stepped out to take a call. That's when Mr. Under-His-Breath (famous for backhanded compliments) stood up and said loudly, "Dianna, with all due respect, we've wasted fifteen minutes. Your product is nothing but a pimple on our back."

My stomach dropped. Then I took a breath and flipped the switch. "If it's a pimple," I said evenly, "it's a profitable one."

I finished the pitch without drama. And did everyone clap? No. But did I leave smaller? Absolutely not. That day, I learned envy dressed up as condescension is just a test of steadiness, and I passed.

What they didn't know is that their words became my workout. Every snide comment was another repetition in perseverance.

GEM: Resilience is flipping the pimple into the power move.

The Truth About Jealousy

People who celebrate your setbacks are usually fighting battles of their own. Their behaviour is their deficit, not yours. And when you can see it that way, their negativity becomes motivation, and you move anyway.

A study found over 80% of people under thirty admit to feeling jealous (Yeung 2022). But we don't need data to know that comparison culture is everywhere. Most of us share the wins and hide the mess, especially on social media, and that type of behaviour creates a gap that breeds envy on every side.

But wanting more doesn't make you selfish. It makes you alive. So, my advice is to be bold. Be brave. And most importantly, be you.

Self-Investment: The Antidote

What you may call selfish, I call it oxygen. Because when you stop investing in yourself, everything else starts fighting for air. You can't pour vision from an empty vessel or inspire a team when you're running on fumes. Growth starts with self-respect, not self-sacrifice.

When you invest in your skills, your health, or your craft, you quiet the comparison voice at the root and raise the bar for everyone you lead. Your courage gives others permission to expand, too.

If it builds the future-you and serves the room, it's a yes. Because every dollar, every hour, every ounce of effort you pour into your own development becomes fuel for the people you lead and love.

Ask yourself this right now, "What's the one investment this month that would make me unmistakably more useful?" Book it. Fund it. Protect it.

GEM: Invest in you so you can lift everyone else.

This is the essence of self-investment. Each decision you make to grow becomes a brick in the foundation of your future. The people you lead rely on that growth. When you evolve, they rise with you.

The Permission to be "Selfish"

For years, I avoided that word. It felt sharp and heavy, like something to apologize for. I grew up believing that being generous, kind, and giving were the gold standards, and they are. But no one taught us how dangerous it is to give until we're empty.

Somewhere along the way, women especially got the message that taking care of ourselves meant we were taking something away from others. That if we paused, said no, or set a boundary, we were being difficult or demanding. But being "selfish" in the right way is about stewardship, not greed. It's about protecting the energy and understanding that allow you to lead, create, and love at full capacity.

When Matthew McConaughey reframed selfishness as the space where the "I" meets the "we", something clicked for me (McConaughey 2020). And the more I understood and met my own needs, the more present and generous I became for others.

Self-sourced leaders don't wait for validation or rescue. They build internal power supplies (energy, focus, fortitude) that fuel everyone around them. You can't pour from an empty tank, and you can't lead from one either.

GEM: Protecting your energy isn't selfish. It's leadership in motion. When you manage your power, you magnify your impact.

So, when envy shows up—whether it's someone else judging your priorities or you are judging theirs—remind yourself that self-focus is not self-absorption. It's the discipline of ensuring your light stays on so others can find theirs.

S.T.E.P. - Flip Envy into Empowerment

When envy hits, don't over think it. Just S.T.E.P. through it:

S   Spot the Signal: Is this their jealousy or my comparison?

T   Translate it: What value or need is underneath?

E   Expand Identity: Ask the future-you, "What move keeps me honest and moving?"

P   Pivot to service: One act that invests in you and lifts someone else.

This is how envy becomes energy and energy becomes influence.

If You Want to Go Deeper

Notice where envy first learned your name. Maybe it started in childhood, like the first time you were called "bossy" for leading or "teacher's pet" for raising your hand often. You don't have to relive it, but it helps to remember how it felt. Awareness is the doorway to empathy, especially for yourself.

For me, it showed up early. I can still picture the hallway; the concrete tile floors, chipped paint on the walls, and me, clutching a stack of certificates after another school assembly. I should've felt proud. Instead, I felt the sting. The whispers, the eye rolls, the quiet space that opened around me like I'd done something wrong just by trying.

I started to wonder if standing out meant standing alone. So, I toned it down. I smiled smaller, spoke up less, kept my hand halfway raised instead of all the way up. But dimming myself didn't make anyone else brighter. It just made me disappear.

Years later, I realized those were my first lessons in envy; not mine, but theirs. And they became the training ground for perseverance. Because once you've learned to be okay with being "too much," you start to crush it.

That old loneliness fuels me now. It's why I notice the quiet achievers, the ones who feel like they don't quite fit in the room they've already earned their way into. Those are my people.

GEM: The moments that made you feel different were never mistakes. They were your introduction to leadership.

The Switch That Changes Everything

Even the smallest hint of jealousy (a sign, a silence, an eyeroll) can shake us. It's easy to shrink and wonder if we did something wrong to instigate this response. But jealousy is rarely about you. It's about where the other person is on their journey.

When you notice envy, use it as information. Ask, "What's this moment showing me?" and S.T.E.P. into it.

— If it's theirs, set a boundary.

— If it's yours, get curious, then invest.

R.E.A.L. leadership turns emotion into awareness and awareness into action.

Your Pocket Flip-Kit: 3 Key Takeaways

1. Envy is information, not indictment

When jealousy shows up, pause before acting. Ask what it's teaching you about your values, your boundaries, or your unmet needs. Awareness turns reaction into direction.

2. Invest in yourself without apology

Self-investment isn't selfish; it's oxygen. The more you build your skills, energy, and understanding, the more capacity you create to lift others. When you rise, you raise the room.

3. Stay self-sourced

True empowerment starts from within. Guard your energy, honour your truth, and move even when it's noisy. Stay self-sourced to remain unstoppable.

Flip the Switch Moment

It's time! Take a breath. Grab your journal. Let's give ourselves some self-investment time.

1. Spot: Where did envy show up this week (yours or theirs)?

2. Translate: What value or need is hiding underneath?

3. Expand: Ask the future-you, "What move keeps me honest and moving today?"

4. Pivot: Name one self-investment that'll also lift your team or family. Put it on the calendar.

5. Boundary (if theirs): Write the sentence you'll use next time, such as, "When X happens, I do Y." Practice it once out loud.

This framework ties in with the work we're doing on the 6Ps: Self-investment fuels your Playbook; boundaries protect your Person; moving anyway even when envy stings is Perseverance; reigniting your spark when comparison dulls it is your Passion; serving others from that overflow becomes Partnership; and doing it with intention anchors your Purpose. And that's how you carry forward a lasting legacy.

Move Anyway

I still feel that sting when someone minimizes my work. And I still catch myself scrolling and shrinking sometimes. The difference now is, I know what to do with it.

If it's their jealousy, I set a boundary (and I'm getting good at it). If it's my comparison, I invest in myself (and I've invested a lot). Fitness, leadership, influence, speaking, writing, mental health, social media, AI; and the list goes on.

Either way, I move. Because forward motion, no matter how small, is where empowerment lives.

Stay inspired,

CHAPTER 6

Overthinking Stuff?
Silence the Inner Critic

*"Great spirits have always encountered violent
opposition from mediocre minds."*
— Albert Einstein.

**GEM: When you start believing others' opinions over
your own truth, you hand them the pen to your story.**

You've done the inner work. You've faced envy, comparison, and the
quiet moments where it would've been easier to shrink back and play
safe. You've learned how to stand tall in your truth and own your
voice, even when it shakes. That's a big deal! But now comes the level
of growth that really tests how much you trust yourself.

Once you start using that voice out loud, people will have opinions.
And not all of those opinions will be kind, accurate, or even worth
your time. Some will challenge you directly, others will hide behind

silence or sarcasm. And if you're not careful, their noise becomes your soundtrack. And that's when you start doubting your own rhythm.

But sometimes it's not even their words that throw us off. Sometimes, it's the voice in our own head, the one that whispers, "Maybe they're right. Maybe I went too far. Maybe I'm not ready."

Are you letting noise limit you?

The Freedom of Letting Go

It wasn't always easy for me, but today, I believe that there comes a point in your development when you stop trying to prove your worth and start trusting it. Or as I like to say, everyone is entitled to their wrong opinion. And once you embrace that, life gets lighter.

For years, I carried the need to make everyone understand me. I thought that if I just explained it the "right way"—with a little more logic, a little more data, more heart or a little less emotion—they'd finally see what I saw. What I didn't realize was that all that explaining was quietly draining me and was me giving away my power.

When you finally stop trying to control how people see you, you start to move with clarity. Every step becomes an act of trust because you no longer need agreement to validate your direction. You just know.

Overthinking and the Urge to Justify

We've all been there, that moment when the conversation goes sideways. You know your stuff, and you've done your work, yet still, someone challenges you just to see if they can. Maybe they interrupt, roll their eyes, or question your credibility in that polite-but-not-so-polite way. If you're like me, you feel the pull to over-explain and prove your point until you're blue in the face. And yes, sometimes it's about winning them over, but more often it's about convincing yourself that your view still matters.

The moment you feel yourself slipping into over-explanation, pause. Take a breath and remind yourself that your worth isn't on trial.

Stop Overthinking

I used to live in that space. I questioned every move, especially in rooms where I was the only woman at the table. Afterward, I'd replay every meeting in my mind, analyzing every comment, every gesture. I thought being right was the win and that if I could just prove my point well enough, I'd earn the respect I craved.

But it's exhausting trying to be right all the time. And it's even more exhausting trying to be liked for being right. It's a bad playbook; one I had to rewrite.

One day, I caught myself mid-spiral asking, "Did I miss something? Why can't they see what I see? What's wrong with me?" Then I just… stopped. That was the day I realized I wasn't questioning my ideals. I was questioning my right to have them.

You can't control other people's opinions. They have the same right to their own viewpoints as you do to your own. You can't change how they think or how they act, but you can decide not to make their opinions your truth. It's time to stop overthinking and start trusting that your perspective is enough.

We overthink our way out of peace. We replay conversations, re-analyze decisions, and script alternate endings that never actually happen. But understanding isn't found in the replay. It's found in the release. When you stop gripping the moment so tightly, space opens for incredible insight to find you.

That's where mentorship, feedback, and reflection come in handy as mirrors that help you see what's real. The right mentor doesn't tell you who to be; they help you recognize who you already are. Feedback, when filtered through self-awareness instead of fear, becomes direction instead of criticism. And reflection, that quiet conversation between you and your truth which becomes the most powerful leadership meeting you'll ever attend.

Peace is the presence of knowing. And that knowing grows every time you choose to reflect instead of reacting.

The Mentor Moment

I once coached a brilliant executive who'd come out of every meeting feeling deflated. She had the experience, the credentials, and the results, but every time someone challenged her, she'd rush to defend herself. After a few months of watching this pattern, I finally asked, "Why do you always feel the need to explain yourself?"

"Because I don't want people to think less of me for having an opinion."

And there it was, the root of it all. It was the fear of being misunderstood.

"Your viewpoint is your unique lens on the world," I responded, "and it's something to celebrate! What if they're wrong about you? What if your opinion is exactly what's needed in the room?"

Everyone is entitled to their viewpoint, even when it's limited. The win isn't getting them to agree but standing in your truth and saying it anyway.

GEM: Strength lives in clarity, not excuses.

Meet Them Where They Are (and Keep Your Ground)

You don't have to agree to understand. When someone tells you that you're wrong, don't fight for your side. Start by meeting them where *they* are, not where *you* are. This was a mistake I made for years, coming from *my* perspective, *my* point of view, and *my* vision for the future. That seems selfish and limiting, doesn't it?

Instead, I learned how to ask better questions to understand what outcome they're after, what matters most to them, and what they're afraid of losing. When you meet people at their level of understanding and experience, you stop battling for validation and start leading through connection.

GEM: Curiosity opens doors; clarity decides which ones you walk through.

And if after that, you still can't meet them halfway, that's okay too. You've added to your own awareness regardless. And they're entitled to their wrong opinion.

When the Noise Gets Loud

Have you ever been in a role where your inner voice just won't shut up, where it's whispering (sometimes shouting), "You don't belong here," even as everyone around you congratulates you? That was me.

When I stepped into my first national executive role, on paper it looked perfect. Everything I'd worked toward, the title, the responsibility, the team, and the impact I could make. But inside, I felt like I'd snuck into a room I wasn't invited to.

The mumbling started before I even unpacked the boxes in my office. "She's not technical enough," or "She's more about style than substance." I'd hear it in meetings and in passing comments. Do you know that feeling when people don't have to say it directly, because their silence says it for them?

Every night, I'd replay my day like a movie I couldn't stop editing. Every sentence I said, every facial expression I caught; I would pick apart how I laughed, whether I'd interrupted too soon, or if I'd sounded confident enough. It was like having a critic living inside my head with a megaphone.

I remember one night vividly: sitting at my kitchen table long after midnight. The house was quiet, everyone was asleep, and there I was with my laptop open and a bottle of wine beside me. My inbox was empty, but my mind was a disaster. I must have rewritten the same note to my boss five times because I was scared she'd finally realize she made a mistake in hiring me.

That's the part of imposter syndrome no one talks about, being so good at self-doubt that you convince yourself you're fooling everyone else.

The shift happened on a Tuesday morning. I walked into the office exhausted, makeup covering the tiredness and caffeine covering the fear. I was meeting with the president, and I'd rehearsed my talking points so thoroughly, they didn't even sound like me anymore. But when I sat down, something inside me shifted. Instead of nervously performing, I just said, "Can I ask, what made you pick me for this role?"

She smiled and leaned back. "Because you can see what others can't. You have a growth mindset and a track record to prove it. You know the business inside out from our customer's perspective. You connect people with purpose and inspire them to move. That's what we need right now."

That changed everything for me. Unlike what the nay-sayers thought, she didn't hire me to be the most technical. She hired me to keep it R.E.A.L, to create our North Star and connect our people to it. I was hired for the parts of leadership we can't measure on a spreadsheet.

I walked out of her office that day feeling a hundred pounds lighter, like the noise in my head had finally met its match. That was my moment of truth, another one of my flip moments, and it was the day I stopped trying to prove myself.

The whispers didn't stop, but my need to silence them did. Because the moment I stopped quieting myself, everything shifted. And now, when I walk into a room that feels heavy or skeptical, I remind myself of that day and that self-trust is the real promotion.

GEM: The moment you stop performing for approval is the moment you start leading for real.

Your Pocket Flip-Kit: 3 Key Takeaways

1. Trust the voice you've already found

You don't need to earn your right to be in the room—you're already there. Stop rehearsing your worth. Learning to trust the voice you've worked so hard to uncover. The world doesn't need your perfection; it needs your presence.

2. Clarity beats justification

When you explain too much, you dilute your power. Say what you mean, mean what you say, and let that be enough. The moment you stop performing for approval, you start leading for real.

3. Meet people where they are, but don't stay there

You can understand someone without surrendering your truth. Empathy gives you perspective, but conviction gives you direction. Listen deeply, respond clearly, and when needed, walk away without guilt.

> **GEM: Flip the switch on overthinking; your authenticity is the edge that gets you to where the puck is going.**

Every time you choose understanding instead of overthinking, you're exercising the same muscles we've built together—the 6Ps—in real time.

Flip the Switch Moment

Dear Fellow Over-Thinker,

If your mind feels like a browser with 43 tabs open (and 17 of them are frozen), you're not alone. We all go there. But this is your chance to pull the lever from stuck to R.E.A.L.

The Switchboard: Overthinking Reset

1. *Power Up Your Superpowers:*

Write out your skills, quirks, values, and life lessons. Where do they overlap? That's your leadership sweet spot.

> *Flip Tip:* Ask 3 people, "What's the one thing you count on me for?" Write down exactly what they say without editing and no modesty.

2. *Anchor in Your Authenticity:*

List 3 moments in your career when you felt fully yourself, where you were in flow, in joy, and in control. What was happening? Who was around you during those times? What words were used to describe you?

> *Flip Tip:* Keep a "Magic Folder" —screenshots, emails, and notes that remind you of who you are when you forget.

3. Mute the Inner Static:

Write down every self-doubt statement running through your head this week. Then, make two columns: "Evidence For" and "Evidence Against."

Flip Tip: When the "Against" list wins, cross that thought out in black marker. Permanently.

4. Install Your Guiding Stars:

Identify 3 people whose courage and clarity you admire.

Flip Tip: Add them to your inner cabinet. Reach out to one with a genuine question.

5. Flip Challenges into Curiosity Quests:

Take your biggest challenge and brainstorm thirty ways to approach it. Yes, thirty. Your brain will surprise you.

Flip Tip: Around idea ten, you'll get silly. By idea twenty, you'll get creative. By idea thirty, you'll find gold.

6. Build Your Gratitude Fuel Tank:

Every Friday, jot down 3 small wins, no matter how minor.

Flip Tip: For each win, say out loud, "That counts." This teaches your brain to celebrate progress.

— Recent Challenge: How did you navigate it?

— Silent Critics: Who are they? How can you flip their noise into fuel?

— Acting Through Doubt: Recall one time you did it anyway.

— Feedback Filter: Do you defend or grow?

GEM: Reflection without action is just mental clutter. It's the noise that keeps you stuck. Flip the damn switch.

CHAPTER 7

Biased to Bias Aware to Bias Accountable.

"If you want something said, ask a man; if you
want something done, ask a woman."
— *Margaret Thatcher*

GEM: When you lead with purpose, you don't need to announce it—your actions do the talking.

You've learned how to quiet the noise inside and trust your own voice. Now, let's turn that same awareness outward, to the patterns, assumptions, and biases that steer our choices. When you move from biased to bias-aware to bias-accountable, you make cleaner decisions, build deeper trust, and keep your values in motion.

Think about this for a moment: you're on a high-speed train heading toward what you want, but suddenly, there's a hiccup in your thinking. That's bias. We all have it. You're biased. I'm biased. We're all card-carrying members of the bias club. The goal isn't to judge it but to catch it and see the pattern so you can change your move.

As we close the door on overthinking and step into confident action, it's tempting to believe the work is complete. Then bias steps into the frame and asks for your attention. Are you listening? It can be quiet, it can be polite, it can even show up as common sense, yet it still shapes the turn you take next. Don't pretend it's not there. Instead, see it, name it, and choose differently.

GEM: Catch the pattern and change the move.

From Biased to Bias-Aware to Bias-Accountable

The word "bias" can make people tense up, but bias doesn't make you bad. It's simply the human way our brains try to make quick sense of the world. We create shortcuts based on what we've seen, what we've been taught, and what we've lived. Those shortcuts help us move fast, but they can also steer us into old habits that don't match who we are now or the leader we're becoming.

Here is how I see it:

Biased means the pattern is driving you.

Bias Aware means you have caught the pattern in the act - you can name it when it shows up.

Bias Accountable means you do something about it. You change your next move because of what you have noticed.

This is where growth happens! This is how we move from running on autopilot to self-awareness…and ultimately from safety to crushing it.

GEM: Bias alert! Embrace your quirks, break the autopilot, and remember that comfort zones are so last season!

P.A.U.S.E. to Flip Bias in Real Time

Always start with a pause! Use this simple pause framework when you feel a quick judgement forming or a familiar story taking over:

P. **Pause the autopilot.** Say it out loud or in your head; this could be bias.

A. **Ask a counter question.** What evidence challenges my first take?

U. **Understand the stakes.** Who benefits or loses if I'm wrong?

S. **Seek a second lens.** Invite in someone else's view, someone who sees differently.

E. **Execute, then examine.** Make the call, then look back later and note what bias you missed and what you'll do next time.

Keep this within reach because the power is in noticing sooner and choosing better every time.

The Million-Dollar Question

You're the captain of your ship, steering through seas shaped by experience, family, stories, education, culture, and rooms you've walked through. Admitting that these influences exist is like spotting a lighthouse on a foggy night.

Here's the million-dollar question: What is steering your decisions today? Are there ideas you favour too quickly or dismiss too easily? Do you give more weight to a familiar voice and not enough to the quiet one? Take a minute and write a few ideas down without judging yourself for them. The goal is awareness.

Awareness is powerful, but it only changes culture when it meets action. So, the next step is applying it where it counts most, and that's how we hire, promote, and trust.

Once you see the pattern, you can change the step. Bias doesn't have to be the villain. It can be the missing clue that will amplify your development and your impact.

GEM: If you don't change the inputs, you repeat the outcomes.

Recasting the Script in Hiring

Here's how bias often sneaks into hiring. We reach for what feels familiar (likely the last success story, the safe choice, or the candidate who "fits"). It feels comfortable, but comfort is the enemy of innovation. The simple fix is to widen the slate. Change where you look, test for skills and outcomes, and for goodness' sake, to stop reenacting the past. When you do this, teams begin to reflect the world you serve, not just the world you know.

Before you make your next short list, ask one more person to nominate an unexpected candidate, add one fresh source and name the one skill the team is missing rather than the one resume you keep trying to replicate. You'll see how small changes will compound quickly.

Wait…She's the Boss

Picture an industry event with mostly men in the room. I arrive with colleagues. I'm relaxed and ready to connect. Then the silent story starts before anyone can speak. *These must be her bosses.* Until the introduction lands: "Meet our President." There's a familiar wave of raised eyebrows, the awkward smiling, and a quick recovery, the kind you see when people realize their assumptions just got caught red-handed.

Then, there's the comedy of international travel. I walk into a hotel with a male colleague, ready to register and dive into a week of meetings. Without fail, the staff assume I'm his "better half." It's like starring in a sitcom where I'm constantly mistaken for the wife! My colleague, to his credit, quickly corrects them with: *"Actually, she's my boss."* And just when you think it can't get any better, a staff member tries to smooth things over with, *"Well…what's the difference?"* It's in those moments I'm reminded why humour is my best travel companion.

Sometimes, all you can do is laugh. But behind the laughter is a deeper truth: these are real, lived experiences that expose the subtle and often unspoken biases that still shape our world. But their surprise isn't my problem. It's my opportunity to educate by example.

GEM: Every raised eyebrow can become momentum when you keep showing up and keep delivering.

The Bias You Didn't See Coming

Some biases are loud and obvious. Others are quiet and somehow have become disguised as commonplace. One that can live inside healthy, high performing teams is the self-serving bias. This is when we take credit for wins and assign blame for losses to circumstances seemingly out of our control, like climate change, market conditions, geopolitical turmoil, or uncertainty in general.

It's human to self-serve, but it slows growth significantly. When markets are shifting and pressure is real, this habit can truly stall a team that would otherwise be capable of bold, creative moves.

The only way through it is taking ownership. When you choose ownership, you convert energy that was tied up in defense mode into energy that moves the work forward. I invite you to become that movement and own it. Ownership expands the room, and the minute you take responsibility, you invite others to move with you.

We've all felt the moments of uncertainty since the pandemic hit, and I hate to be the one to piss in your cornflakes, but we're leading in a time of sustained perma-crisis. Perma-crisis is defined by the *Harvard Business Review* as a prolonged state of uncertainty where change is constant and instability is the norm (Einhorn 2025). How we adapt to change, how we respond to it, and the questions we ask ourselves before making decisions have never been more critical.

The world of perma-crisis demands filling war rooms way before the war hits, with innovative options and proactive out-of-the-box, "go-to-market" strategies built in preparation for, not reactive to. In these moments, teams have the chance to either struggle or excel together by coming together with bold optimism and navigating the unknown, owning every step they take.

One of the most profound learnings in my career emerged during what seemed like an insurmountable challenge. It not only shaped my momentum but also strengthened my confidence in leading through chaos and uncertainty, a crucial skill I cherish and continue to fine tune in today's uncertain times.

The Power of Owning Your Part

Years ago, I sat across from a client whose insurance claim had just been denied. And it wasn't a small number. Frustration filled the room, and it would've been easy to point at the policy, at the wording, at the process, or at the insurance carrier. Instead, I asked myself the only question that mattered: *Did I do enough to make the exclusions clear? Did I ask the deeper questions about the business so I could see the risks that hadn't yet surfaced?*

The honest answer was, not quite. I told the client exactly that, and I asked for a chance to do better right now, not later. We sat on the same side of the table and looked at options together. Then, when I went back to the insurer, I was transparent about what we could have done better, and I asked for partnership to make the client whole. Because we'd invested in trust over time, they agreed. We resolved it, we changed our process, we trained our team to translate policy into plain language, and we built deeper questions into our discovery so the hidden risks would show up before they cost someone everything.

That day reinforced what I believe. Owning my gap built trust I couldn't have developed any other way. We turned what could've been a fracture into a fix and made the fix a part of how we worked.

GEM: Owning my gaps turns friction into a fix and trust into momentum.

Today's Constant Change

In logistics and in many industries, conditions can shift without warning. Weather, policy, world events, and capacity all play their part. When promises aren't met, the first move is often to point outward. A stronger move is to ask, what could we have communicated earlier, what options did we fail to surface, what step can we take now that restores trust.

This is where bias awareness and accountability meet. You notice the story you want to tell, you choose the truth, and you act in a way that strengthens the relationship rather than explains it away. And bias doesn't clock out when we leave the office. It follows us home in how we love, how we listen, and how we learn from difference.

The Gift of Perspective

Bias finds a way into the most personal corners of our lives. My life and leadership have been shaped by difference and by love. My marriage brought me into a new cultural lens that widened my own, and growing up with a mother who led through a hearing impairment taught me to listen with my eyes and my heart.

These experiences continue to expand my perspective at home and at work.

This work is where awareness becomes integrity. When you flip the switch on bias, you don't just avoid mistakes but create spaces where different voices feel safe to contribute, where creativity can breathe, and where performance grows in much the same way as people do.

Your Pocket Flip-Kit: 3 Key Takeaways

1. Everyone has bias.

Awareness is strength, not shame.

2. P.A.U.S.E. before you decide.

Think twice, then act once.

3. Accountability builds trust.

Owning your gaps turns friction into fuel.

Bias Cue: P.A.U.S.E. in Practice

Here's how to use it in the moment:

- Pause the autopilot.

- Ask the counter question.

- Understand the stakes.

- Seek a second lens.

- Execute, then examine.

Write it on a sticky note and keep it where you make decisions. Bias awareness isn't a one time clean up. It's a daily practice that keeps you honest, agile, and aligned.

Flip the Switch Moment

Grab your journal, your favourite pen, and get ready to become a little uncomfortable as we dive into our bias portfolio, because we're all card-carrying members.

Power Pause: Be Bias-Aware Self-Assessment

Goal: Move from unconscious influence to intentional and fair decision making.

How to use this tool:

1. Think of a real situation (past or present) where you need to make a decision or assess a person, group, or idea. Got one in mind? Write it down at the top of your page.

2. Read each question below and score yourself from 1–5:

    — 1 = not at all true for me right now

    — 3 = somewhat true or mixed awareness

    — 5 = very true, or I actively do this

3. Total your score at the end for your Bias-Awareness Level.

The Bias-Awareness Assessment (Score each from 1–5)

______**Assumption Check:** What assumptions am I making here, and are they based on verified facts or stereotypes?

______**Perspective Filter:** How might my own background or experiences be colouring my view of this situation?

______**Confirmation Bias Detector:** Am I only seeking evidence that supports my existing view, or am I genuinely open to other perspectives?

______**Emotional Clarity:** What feelings are surfacing for me right now, and could they be influencing my judgment?

______**Listening Depth:** Have I listened, really listened, to people who might see this differently than I do?

______**Openness to Change:** Am I willing to change my mind if new credible information comes to light?

______**Ripple Effect Awareness:** Have I considered who else might be affected by this decision, and how?

______**Experience Relevance Check:** Am I leaning too heavily on past experiences that might not apply in this context?

______**Fairness Meter:** Have I ensured my decision is fair, inclusive, and considers multiple viewpoints?

______**Bias Guardrails:** Do I have personal strategies in place to catch and challenge my biases before making final decisions?

______**TOTAL SCORE**

Scoring:

41–50: Bias-Accountable. You're highly aware and intentional. Consider mentoring others in bias awareness.

31–40: Bias-Aware. You recognize bias but still have some blind spots to explore.

21–30: Bias in the Shadows. Bias is influencing you more than you think. Slow down and review your habits.

10–20: Bias on Auto Pilot. Decisions are likely driven more by unexamined bias. This is definitely your switch-flip moment.

Action commit, write it now:

One bias I'll watch this week is ____________.

One P.A.U.S.E. step I'll practice is ____________.

One person I'll ask for a second lens is ____________.

Spark Questions:

— Which question(s) did you score lowest on, and why?

— In the last month, can you recall a situation where a bias influenced you, and what you would do differently now?

— What's one practical "bias interrupter" you can put in place immediately (e.g., asking someone with an opposite viewpoint to weigh in before you decide)?

Bias awareness helps you see what's shaping your choices. But once you can see the pattern, the next question is, what's shaping you? That's where the deeper work begins, the work of mastering your thoughts. Bias may influence your perception, but your thoughts define your reality. So, when you take ownership of both, you stop reacting to the world and start designing it.

CHAPTER 8

Master Your Thoughts, Master your World

*"Change your thoughts,
and you change your world."*
— *Norman Vincent Peale.*

GEM: What you feed your mind becomes your life.

You've learned to see the patterns that shape your choices. You've identified how to spot your bias and choose differently. Now, it's time to take that awareness one step further—inward—and unlock infinite possibility!

Mastering your thoughts is the next level of flipping the switch, because what you focus on becomes the lens through which you see everything else. Just as bias quietly steers perception, your thoughts quietly shape your reality.

Your thoughts are the quiet architects of your destiny. They're always building, even when you're not paying attention. So, when you take control of them, you reclaim your direction. You also build your confidence and your power to create the future you actually want. This is where personal empowerment stops being a concept and starts becoming your daily practice.

Too often, we inhabit a world where what we don't desire takes control of our focus, creating a cycle of negativity that mirrors our inner thoughts. The saying "Where your focus goes, energy flows," heralded by Tony Robbins (Robbins 2024), captures it perfectly.

So, pause and ask yourself: what are you thinking about today? What you focus on, you attract. Yet we tend to focus on what we don't want, then wonder why it keeps showing up. Maybe your mind replays the frustrations of the day (like that driver who cut you off, the rising energy bills, the colleague who drains your energy, or the client who just doesn't get it). When your mind is full of noise, everything starts to feel dull and heavy.

But you hold the power to shift that perspective. By intentionally owning your thoughts, you can reset your frame of mind and step onto a path that's full of possibility. This is your invitation to flip the switch from reaction to creation.

Instead of focusing on what's gone wrong, focus on the solutions. Imagine the power of attraction as your personal rehearsal for the future you want to create. By consistently rehearsing who you want to become (your future self), you align your thoughts, your behaviours, and energy with that vision. It's like creating a mental blueprint for your dreams, drawing them closer with every thought.

So, now that you know what to do, step into the role of your future self today and watch how quickly opportunity begins to align!

GEM: Don't fake it. Live it in advance!

My 90-Second Future Self Ritual

Every morning, I take ninety seconds to rehearse my future self. I close my eyes and picture the person I'm becoming: stronger, calmer, happier, healthier, more influential, more grounded, and spiritual. I imagine the sound of her voice, the calm in her body, the joy in her stride. Then I take one small action that matches her energy that day.

Your brain responds to vivid rehearsal. When you practice a state on purpose, it becomes easier to live it in real time. The subconscious doesn't distinguish between what's real and what's rehearsed. It simply follows your focus.

If you give it clear direction, it'll get to work bringing it to life.

The Hardest Flip: Mastering Your Own Story

Do you remember your high school years? The butterflies, the first crush, the feeling that every little thing mattered? For me, that crush was a boy named Ken. I was fifteen. He was eighteen and captain of the football team, with blonde hair and blue eyes. He was the guy every girl seemed to want, so naturally, I found myself inventing excuses to cross his path.

I moved my locker closer to his, hung around his hallway, and convinced my friends to sit near his table at lunch. Looking back, it sounds so dramatic, but I was just a teenager chasing possibility.

Then came the twist. I showed up at my part-time job at the local grocery store, and there he was, bagging groceries at the next checkout. Fate had a sense of humour; suddenly, he was a part of my daily life!

Weeks went by in a blur. We started talking more, laughing more, and before long, he asked me out to a movie. For a fifteen-year-old, it felt like winning the lottery. Until my dad—a teacher at my school—reminded me of his very clear rule: no dating until I was sixteen. And that was that.

Even then, I noticed something powerful. What we focus on tends to expand. I'd poured my energy into this one idea, this one person, and somehow, the universe rearranged itself to make it real. And as I got older, I realized that same pattern showed up everywhere. When I set my mind toward something and focused with intention, doors opened. Call it the power of attraction or simply disciplined focus. Whatever it's called, it works.

Winning scholarships, leading high-performing teams, earning leadership roles I once thought were out of reach—none of these things were accidents. They were the outcome of focus, belief, and consistent action.

Becoming a CEO in my thirties, and the first female President for Canada in a major global firm, was proof that what you rehearse in your mind eventually finds its way into your reality.

Take a moment and ask yourself, "What if you focused higher? What if you dreamed bigger? What if your next chapter started sooner? Those questions are the invitation. The universe loves a decisive mind.

***GEM: Think big, because size does matter,
but only in your dreams and impact.***

The Power of Attraction in Action

Take a quick inventory of your thoughts. What's on repeat? What worries or frustrations are you replaying that no longer deserve space in your mind? What you dwell on becomes what you attract. So, are you fixating on the limits? Or are you creating room for bigger dreams and bolder moves?

Your mind is powerful. The stories you allow to loop inside it will shape the direction of your life. Choose them wisely.

Over the past decade, I've been more intentional than ever about using what I call my superpower (the power of attraction). I think big and amplify what I value most: connection. When I want something deeply, I don't leave it as a wish. I write it down, I say it out loud, and I picture it vividly. I act as if it already belongs in my life.

That's how this book began. For years, I told myself I should write it. Then one day, my daughter said, "Mom, you need to take your own advice. Stop saying you should write a book someday and make that someday today." That moment flipped my switch. And the exciting truth is, clarity attracts opportunity, but only when you're bold enough to make the first move. Writing this book wasn't just about putting words on paper but about stepping into my purpose.

I courageously reached out to one of my lifelong mentors and bestselling authors, Jeffrey Gitomer (the King of Sales), and asked him to coach me through the process. But before I messaged him, I outlined my intent, my audience, and my chapter map. I was ready. Thirty minutes later, he replied. And within a month, I was in his Charlotte studio, building the blueprint for this book.

It felt surreal but deeply right. And it's proof that when focus meets purpose, and you take bold action, doors open.

GEM: Bold asks open unexpected doors. When focus meets purpose, connection turns into opportunity.

From Someday to Today

You've seen what happens when focus meets purpose. Now, ask yourself: What dream have you tucked away, waiting for the magical thing called "someday?" Rarely does the time ever feel perfect, so what if you decided that today was the day?

Write down your top fifty dreams—yes, fifty. Don't edit, don't limit, just write. Then narrow them down to ten that align with your first three Ps (Person, Purpose, and Passion).

From those, choose one—the one that sets your soul on fire. Say it out loud. Visualize it. Then act on it. Dreams don't come alive through waiting; they come alive through movement. Step into your intention, flip the switch, and start walking toward it today.

GEM: Stop waiting for someday. Today is the day to flip the switch on the dream that sets your soul on fire.

Let's capture the essence before you take this into your own daily rituals.

Your Pocket Flip-Kit: 3 Key Takeaways

1. Thoughts set direction

You can't control every circumstance, but you can choose every thought. Ensure the thoughts you give space in your mind are aimed toward the things you desire.

2. Rehearse, then act

Belief builds momentum through repetition. Start with mental rehearsals, then move into actively taking action in the real-world.

3. One bold ask beats ten quiet wishes

Focus with courage, and the right doors open.

GEM: Master your thoughts and you master your world.

Flip the Switch Moment

Grab your journal, play music that inspires you, and get ready to fuel your fire.

1. Fuel for the Fire: Using the 6Ps Model to Reach Your Big Scary Dream

Your big dream is the kind that makes your heart race and your palms sweat. It's the kind that stretches you far beyond your comfort zone while lighting you up inside. It's the one your future self will thank you for.

Let's test-drive the 6P Model to turn attraction into daily action. Grab a pen and maybe some colourful markers or sticky notes, but before you begin, clearly write down your big scary dream. Define it. Get a little creative too and give it a name!

2. Your Person (Mind / Body / Spirit)

Fuel your inner world so your outer world transforms.

— **Mindfulness Minute:** Spend ninety seconds in stillness, focusing on your breath. Clear the mental noise so your dream has room to breathe.

— **Positivity Audit:** List three things you'll add to your life to bring more joy, and three things you'll remove to protect your energy and preserve your peace.

— **Journal Prompt:** "How will I strengthen my mind, body, and spirit to become the version of me, my future self, who lives my big scary dream?"

3. Your Purpose (Your Why)

Anchor your actions in what truly matters to you.

— **Value Map:** Write down your top five values and one action this week that honours each.

— **Future Self Visualization:** Picture the version of you who's already achieved it.

— **Journal Prompt:** "What would my future self thank me for if I started today?"

4. Your Passion (Your Rocket Fuel)

Turn emotion into momentum.

— **Affirmations:** Write three "I am" statements about your dream-achiever self (e.g., "I'm bold and unstoppable," "I'm magnetic to opportunity," "I'm thriving in my big scary dream").

— **Vision Board Sprint:** Fill it with images and words that capture your dream.

— **Journal Prompt:** "What lights me up so much that it makes chasing my big scary dream irresistible?"

5. Your Playbook (Your Roadmap)

Map the daring path to your big dream.

— Break your dream into three bold milestones.

— Under each milestone, list three micro-steps you can take this month.

— Celebrate each one.

— **Journal Prompt:** "What's the very next action I can take to get closer to my big scary dream?"

6. Your Perseverance (Your Fortitude)

Train your thoughts to be your ally.

— **Thought Flip:** When doubt says, "I can't," flip it into "I can, and I will—here's how."

— **Gratitude Shift:** Write down 3 wins each night.

— **Journal Prompt:** "What fear can I flip into fierce determination right now?"

Your Partnerships (Your Network / Community)

Build the dream team around your big dream.

— **Inner Cabinet:** List five people who lift you up and believe in your vision.

— **Ask:** "How can we help each other move closer to our goals?"

— **Journal Prompt:** "Who can I connect with this week to build momentum?

Flip Tip: Pair your ninety-second future self ritual with this model. Every morning, step into the version of you who already lives the dream. Then take one real-world action that matches it.

When your thoughts align with who you're becoming, your energy shifts, and the people around you can feel it. But before you fully *become*, you must unbecome. Sometimes the most powerful switch you can flip is the one that turns off everything that isn't you.

CHAPTER 9

Unbecoming...
Subtract to Become

"Maybe the journey isn't so much about becoming anything. Maybe it's about un-becoming everything that isn't really you, so you can be who you were meant to be in the first place."
— *Paulo Coelho.*

GEM: There's no greater reward than living the life only you can live.

Becoming isn't always adding more. Sometimes, it's the courage to set things down.

You've learned to focus your thoughts and aim your actions. Now, the next flip isn't forward but inward. Mastering your thoughts was about building clarity. Here, you need to create space for it.

Unbecoming is the work of setting down expectations, titles, and old stories that keep you performing instead of being. Think of a sculptor standing in front of a big block of stone. The masterpiece isn't added. It's revealed. That is your journey now, chiseling away what doesn't belong so the real you can lead without apology. Subtract to become.

Unbecoming is the moment you recognize what you took on to survive or to succeed and decide what stays (and what goes). Every layer you strip away brings you closer to the person you were always meant to be.

The Journey Inward

When the world went quiet during COVID-19, so did I. It was uncomfortable at first, with no meetings, no planes, no noise to hide behind. The stillness felt awkward, almost itchy, like standing in an unfamiliar room. But then questions I'd been dodging for years started whispering louder, and I filled journals with thoughts and ideas, hungry for truth instead of busyness.

Life looked fine on the surface—a marriage I loved, a family that grounded me, and a career that challenged me—but underneath was a tug, a quiet pull toward something deeper. I needed to uncover what was waiting to come alive.

Have you ever felt that? That nudge that quietly whispers, "There's more to you than this." Write it down when it shows up. Sometimes, naming it is the first step to hearing yourself again.

Layers I Set Down

Growing up Roman Catholic gave me a clear script for goodness that didn't always leave room for my voice. Being the eldest daughter of a mother who led fiercely through hearing loss taught me perseverance but also handed me quiet pressure to echo her strength. A painful custody battle left scars I carried long after the papers were signed, and years in male-dominated boardrooms shaped a version of me that often didn't fit.

None of these erased me, but together they layered on expectations that blurred my edges. Unbecoming meant setting down what was borrowed and keeping what was true, for me. And for the first time, I could hear my own thoughts before the world's opinions crowded in.

What I wanted most wasn't more success; it was more time. Time to breathe, to choose, to live aligned with what mattered. That longing sent me deeper, and I asked myself not what I wanted to do but why it mattered to me.

7 Levels Deep - Finding My "Why"

To cut through the noise, I used a simple but powerful tool from Dean Graziosi called 7 Levels Deep (Graziosi 2019). In this exercise, you ask one question seven times: why is this important to me? And each layer gets you closer to the one that matters.

Here's how my exercise looked after much reflection:

1. Why is time so important to me? Because time is finite. If I can win it back, I can have more freedom.

2. Why is freedom so important to me? Freedom means choice, and I hate feeling stuck. I want my choices to align with who I really am.

3. Why is choice so important to me? Choice lets me pursue joy. When I live in alignment, I feel happy and alive.

4.   Why is joy so important to me? Joy is more than emotion; it's one of my core values. When I live in joy, I'm my truest self, and that positivity becomes contagious.

5.   Why is positive influence so important to me? Because the power of positivity is its ability to create an impact of empowerment. I love empowering others to do more and dream more!

6.   Why is empowering others so important to me? Because when people thrive, businesses, families, and communities thrive.

7.   Why is creating environments for people to thrive so important to me? Because this is my life's purpose. This is why I get up every day. I live and breathe inspiring the lives of others. Living without purpose would be my greatest regret.

GEM: A life without purpose is the one regret I refuse to carry.

This is a masterclass exercise in learning how to subtract to become. Each "why" carved away what wasn't mine to carry. This experience didn't add new goals to my list, but it did strip away the noise. It reminded me that purpose isn't about collecting achievements but serving through authenticity and intention. Each "why" brought me closer to the truth until I could finally say, *this is me. This is why I'm here.*

Living the Lesson

Once I uncovered my core purpose, everything else shifted. I stopped chasing milestones and started honouring meaning in my life.

When an industry award arrived, what hit me the hardest was a mentor's comment left for me on LinkedIn: "You are a role model in a space where words fight for attention and where actions become the only differentiator." I wasn't performing Dianna anymore. I was simply *being* her. And other people could feel the difference.

Awards fade, but alignment with your core truth will stay with you.

GEM: Embrace the journey, honour the way, and let living as your true self be the celebration that outlasts every milestone.

Your Pocket Flip-Kit: 3 Key Takeaways

Capture the core before you move: three reminders to keep you honest when old habits start calling on you again.

1. Subtract to become.

Growth isn't about collecting more. It's about setting down what no longer serves you. Every "no" makes room for what's true.

2. Your Purpose isn't found. It's remembered.

Purpose lives beneath the noise. The more you peel away other people's expectations, the clearer your own "why" becomes.

3. Being is the real becoming.

When you stop performing for approval and start leading from alignment, you shift from trying to prove your worth to simply living it. That's where your influence deepens and your peace begins.

GEM: Unbecoming is liberation, not loss. Every layer you release brings you home to you.

Flip the Switch Moment

Grab your journal, settle in, and let your thoughts flow. Ask yourself the honest, probing questions: *What do I really want? What do I truly desire?*

The 7-Levels Deep Exercise

It's like peeling back an onion. Use this method to dive deep beyond the surface level thinking you're used to. Keep asking, "Why is this important to you?" until you unearth the core of your purpose. Have fun and see where this exercise takes you!

To get started: What do you want more of? And why is that important to you? This starts the first level. Then continue the exercise to complete the chart.

Why is __________ so important to me?	
Why is __________ so important to me?	
Why is __________ so important to me?	
Why is __________ so important to me?	
Why is __________ so important to me?	
Why is __________ so important to me?	
Why is __________ so important to me?	

Your Purpose / Your Soul Level Mission:

____

Now bring it to life:

— One layer I'll set down this week is

____

— One action that matches my purpose is

____

— One person I'll tell, to keep myself accountable, is

____

Take a deep breath when you finish. What you've uncovered here has been waiting under the noise, and you've just chiseled it free.

Once you remember who you are, every decision that follows becomes simpler, because now you are choosing from truth instead of fear. Becoming isn't ahead of you but underneath. Subtract to become; shed what isn't you, and lead from what is.

CHAPTER 10

Mutual Trust – The Quiet Edge

*"To be trusted is a greater compliment
than being loved"*
—George MacDonald

GEM: Trust isn't just a compliment. It's the deepest form of respect and the greatest gift. When people trust you, they're betting on your potential, and that belief can move mountains.

You've shed what isn't you. You've done the deep work to uncover your why, and you've stripped down what no longer fits. Now, it's time to lead from what *is* you. Mutual trust is the steady agreement between two people to tell the hard truth, show they care, keep the promise, and bring the skill, especially when it's hard. Trust is that quiet pulse beneath every relationship you build, every decision you make, and every moment of leadership.

When people ask what drives me, my answer is always "connection." Connection is my oxygen. But connection without trust is impossible. It's like a bridge without anchors. It might look solid for a while, but one strong wind, and it's gone.

Trust is our truest currency. It's how we build safety, earn the loyalty of others, and make courage contagious.

When the World Stopped, We Saw What Stayed

When the world slowed down, leadership was under a bright, unforgiving microscope. The pandemic stripped away the stage lights and revealed what had quietly expired. Some led with fear and control, trying to manage the uncertainty by tightening their grip. Others led with empathy and humility. And the difference was impossible to miss. It was written in faces on Zoom calls, in voices that sighed from exhaustion, and in the silence that followed bad news, but also in the warmth of someone saying, "Hey, are you okay?" for the first time all week.

For a moment, the walls between work and life disappeared. Leaders were no longer walking the polished hallways or sitting in rich corporate offices. We were being welcomed into living rooms, kitchens, basements, and makeshift desks beside piles of LEGO and math homework and getting camera-bombed by pets.

I joined a call one morning, still in my slippers, and one of my team members was juggling a toddler on her lap while leading a discussion with more focus and grace than most boardrooms ever see. This is what leadership looks like. It's not presentation decks or talking points but presence. It's showing up as R.E.A.L. as humanly possible.

The leaders who showed up with empathy and humanity earned a kind of trust that no title or bonus could buy.

GEM: Trust is the only real currency of business and life. Without it, everything stalls. But with it, everything scales.

The Currency that Never Loses Value

Trust currency compounds every time you follow through, tell the truth, or admit when you've missed the mark. You can also feel the trust bank grow or drain in real time.

In a culture without trust, people whisper more than they speak. Ideas start shrinking and fear takes the front row seat in every department. In a culture built on trust, people move freely between departments, across levels, and beyond titles. They collaborate more, they challenge each other and their leaders, they create new solutions, and they believe in a brighter future—together.

When I look back on my own journey, every defining moment (the promotions, the changes, even the failures), it all came down to trust:

— Who trusted me enough to give me a shot.

— Who I trusted enough to tell the truth to.

And whether I trusted myself enough to keep going when things felt impossible.

Trust isn't one-dimensional. It's not something you have or don't have. It's something you build, moment by moment, and you do this by how you show up when it matters most.

A Leadership Moment of Reflection - Post-COVID

When I stepped into a new leadership role after the pandemic, I stood at a crossroads. The world had changed, people had changed, and leadership had to change with it. Overnight, the playbook became outdated. What once worked (the structures, controls, and predictability from past market trends) suddenly felt hollow. I had to ask myself, "What kind of leader do I want to be for my team, and for all of us, in this moment that will define so much of what comes next?"

Trust is the heartbeat of modern leadership. Full stop. If mutual trust was truly one of my core values (which it absolutely was), I needed to be intentional about how I built it every day—and honest about how I might be eroding it without realizing it.

In the past, I had moments of over-promising to keep the peace, under-listening when people needed to be heard, and rushing hard conversations because slowing down felt too vulnerable. I was so focused on holding it all together at times, I missed the pauses where real growth and alignment actually happen. And when I eventually realized this, it cut deep, but it also released me. It reminded me that true leadership isn't found in control or composure but in the courage to listen, to pause, and lead with presence.

Leadership has little to do with hitting KPIs or checking boxes on a 90-day plan. That's *management*. Leadership is integrity in motion that leaves a room safer, braver, and more inspired, purely because you were there.

The question that still fuels me today is, how do I create an impact that lasts beyond the results in front of me, even beyond my own expiration date? The impact that outlives you is built in how people feel and how they behave when you're not in the room.

So, what mark do you want to leave?

Your current role will evolve or end one day. It's inevitable. But something even greater, if you choose to attract it, will be waiting when you have that opportunity to flip the switch. The question is, what will you leave behind that lives and breathes and carries forward beyond you?

Maybe your legacy is a culture reset that lets people speak freely. Maybe it's a joy or wellness ritual that inspires balance and happiness across your team. Maybe it's creating a space people feel seen. Whatever it is, name it, focus on it, and breathe life into it where you stand today.

For me, that legacy is mutual trust. Mutual trust feels like two people moving in sync, confident neither will let the other fall. Have you ever worked with someone who made you feel that safe and stretched? The kind of leader who believes in you so deeply, you rise just to meet their faith in you? That's the power of mutual trust. It's the quiet assurance that lets people take bold steps because they know they'll be caught instead of blamed.

My understanding of mutual trust came from life. I've broken it, rebuilt it, and been blindsided by it, just like you. And each scar taught me something that trust needs a blueprint. Without care and consistency, even the best intentions fall apart.

When mutual trust is strong, people speak up and progress flows. When it's weak, fear fills the cracks. The choices that build it are rarely big ones. They're the small, steady acts that compound over time.

GEM: Legacy isn't what you build. It's what others keep building after you've left the room; what carries forward even once it's out of your own hands.

Big words don't build trust, but our daily choices do. Here's the blueprint I carry into every room.

The Blueprint of Mutual Trust in Motion: H.E.R.S.

Four anchors make trust feel real: Honesty (truth), Empathy (care), Reliability (follow-through), and Skill (competence).

Honesty

Honesty is where trust begins, and sometimes where it's rebuilt. It's not the big declarations that matter but the quiet truth-telling in moments when silence would be easier. Early in my leadership, I thought being honest meant delivering the tough messages fast. Now, I know it also means naming what I don't know and inviting others to the solution. When people see you tell the truth—even when it costs you comfort—that's when they believe you.

Empathy

Empathy is seeing the person before the performance. It's asking, "What might they be carrying right now?" instead of "What's wrong with them?" It's pausing long enough to listen without fixing. People don't remember your perfect answers, but they remember when they felt understood. Being understood is the permission people need to risk again.

Reliability

Reliability is where credibility lives! It's following through on the small promises like returning the call, showing up on time, or keeping your word when no one is keeping score. In leadership, consistency builds safety. People can handle bad news, but what they can't handle is unpredictability in how you show up. Reliability is how you say "you can count on me" without ever saying the words.

Skill:

Skill is the confidence behind the connection. It's knowing your craft, staying curious, and committing to growth so you can back your heart with competence. People may trust your intentions, but they stay when they trust your ability. For me, skill is about being prepared, not perfection. It's showing your team that you care enough to stay sharp, evolve, and lead with both humility and mastery. Care is a skill, and mastery is how you prove it. Your heart opens the door, and your skill keeps people in the room.

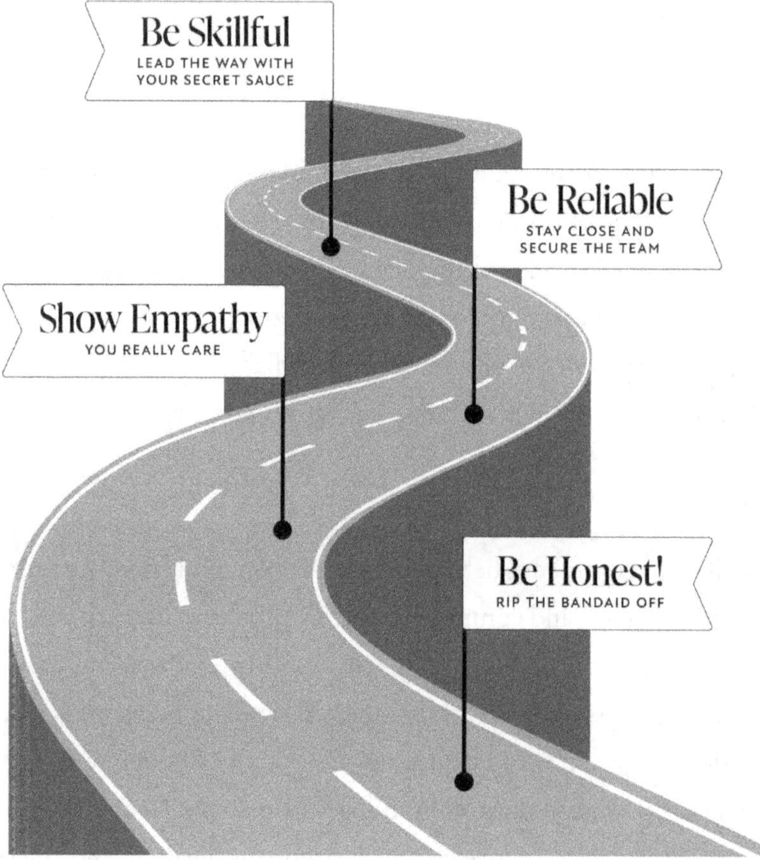

Together, these four anchors create a rhythm people can feel. Together, they turn values into velocity. When you lead through H.E.R.S. trust becomes the current and the dance that brings everyone through it.

GEM: Trust isn't built by words or titles. It's built by the steady rhythm of how you show up, day after day.

Culture is Built in the Hard Moments

The truest test of leadership never arrives with a calendar invite. It shows up when you least suspect it. You can plan strategy sessions and paint values on the wall, but culture isn't built there. It's built in the hallway after bad news. It's built in the silence that follows a mistake. It's built in the way people look at each other when something goes wrong, and everyone's wondering what happens next.

For me, that test came shortly after stepping into that new leadership role in the post-pandemic world. An operational failure in one of our largest business areas sent shockwaves through the company. Customers were frustrated, teams were stretched, and the tension was thick enough to feel in every conversation. The old culture would've defaulted to blame or consequence management (find the problem, find the person, and move on). But I'd promised myself, and my team, we'd lead differently.

So, we gathered the team, and we told the truth. I stood in front of that group, feeling the weight of the room, as I said, "We're not here to blame. We're here to learn and fix it fast together."

For a long moment, it was quiet. Then one person spoke up. "Okay. Then here's what happened." Honesty lowered the temperature in the room and curiosity stepped in to raise the standard.

That was the turning point which allowed us to flip the switch on the company culture. One person's courage gave everyone else permission to speak. And within hours, the truth surfaced, ideas flowed, and people at all levels of the organization (who'd stayed silent for months) started leaning into each other. What could have divided us ended up connecting us.

By the end of the week, the issue was fixed, but more importantly, our people saw that mistakes weren't career-ending and that trust became the heartbeat of our culture.

GEM: Fail fast. Fail forward. Keep learning and keep moving!

H.E.R.S. Beyond the Boardroom

The same principles that strengthen teams can also balance you when life feels unrecognizable.

In 2007, my "year of the hat trick," I was juggling divorce, relocation, motherhood, and a new career chapter. I didn't yet understand that self-trust is the foundation of every other kind, so I was trying to be perfect instead of being real. But that year taught me that the hardest leadership work we'll ever do is in the quiet moments of our lives when no one's watching.

Honesty

Back then, honesty would've meant admitting that I was tired and scared, not pretending I could handle it all. The truth I avoided was the one that could've set me free. "I'm not okay, and I need help."

What's the truth you're avoiding right now that needs your honesty?

Empathy

Empathy would've meant giving myself grace instead of guilt. It's easy to offer compassion to others, but much harder to extend it inward when you feel like you should have it all together.

Where in your life could you use a little more empathy from you today?

Reliable Support

Reliability would have meant keeping promises to myself (e.g., sleeping more, eating better, carving out quiet time) instead of breaking them to meet everyone else's expectations.

What support do you need right now that you're too proud to ask for?

Skill

Skill would've meant creating structure in the storm. Building simple boundaries, celebrating small wins, asking for help from those who'd walked this road before me. Skillful action comes down to intention.

What action could you take today that would make tomorrow easier?

Looking back, had I lived the H.E.R.S model then, some of those nights might have felt less heavy. But those same lessons now shape every decision I make. They remind me that trust begins at home and moves into the office through how you talk to yourself, how you forgive yourself, and how you keep showing up even when it gets messy.

***GEM: The trust you build with yourself
sets the standard for every relationship
and every result that follows.***

Mutual trust is what opens the door to deeper relationships, inspires new ideas, and builds spaces where people feel safe to bring their best. It creates environments for everyone to thrive in, especially you.

Your Pocket Flip-Kit: 3 Key Takeaways

1. Trust starts inside.

If you can't rely on yourself, no one else truly can.

2. Mutual beats one-way.

Give trust, receive trust, and protect it fiercely—especially when it's tested.

3. H.E.R.S. keeps it R.E.A.L.

Honesty, empathy, reliability and skill turn intention into integrity.

**GEM: Titles expire, but trust doesn't.
Build the kind that outlives you.**

Flip the Switch Moment

Take a deep breath and grab your journal. It's your turn to flip the switch and bring H.E.R.S. to life.

Self Check:

Where are you asking for trust but not earning it today? Write one area down, personally or professionally.

Mirror Reflection:

Who needs to hear you say, "You can count on me," this week? What promise to yourself have you quietly broken?

H.E.R.S. in Action:

Choose one of the four anchors and apply it intentionally today. Maybe it's honesty in a tough conversation, empathy with someone under pressure, reliability in a small follow-up, or skill in preparing for a moment that matters. Notice what changes when you lead through this lens immediately.

The Quiet Work of Trust

Trust isn't a milestone you reach but a muscle you build. Every time I've lost it, rebuilt it, or chosen it when it felt risky, it's shaped how I lead and how I've lived my life.

The moments that tested me most like the failures, the heartbreaks, the honest conversations that made my voice shake are the ones that refined me.

If this chapter leaves you with anything, let it be this:

— Keep showing up with honesty even when it's hard.

— Offer empathy even when you're tired.

— Remain reliable when no one's watching.

— And use skill that reflects your care.

Because trust, real mutual trust, will keep the lights on for you when everything else goes dark. And that's a switch worth flipping every day.

Stay inspired,

CHAPTER 11

Culture Moves When Star Teams Lead

"Until I came to IBM, I probably would have
told you that culture was just one among several
important elements in any organization's makeup
and success…I came to see, in my time at IBM,
that culture isn't just one aspect of the game,
it is the game".
— Louis V. Gerstner Jr.

**GEM: Culture is a business's oxygen.
Strategy can't breathe without it.**

You've built trust at the human level, now scale it. This is where your inner alignment becomes everyone's advantage. When you build a culture on mutual trust and star teams, results follow without needing to be chased.

Strategies shift and plans will change, but culture decides whether your people rise or retreat. Culture is the heartbeat that fuels mutual trust, it empowers star teams and inspires ordinary individuals to achieve extraordinary results. You can't fake it or force it—you have to live it.

The leaders we remember, the ones we actually want to follow, aren't the ones with the fancy titles or the biggest offices. They're the ones who earn trust, build connections, and leave imprints on our hearts and minds. They show us what's possible. Which is why every time you choose honesty over hiding, empathy over ego, reliability over excuses, and skillful action over passivity, you ignite trust and unlock possibilities.

This path isn't polished, but it is powerful. It's shaped by hard work, honest "aha" moments, and consistent growth. Trust the process, take this moment to truly honour your evolution, and lead like you were meant to. When you do, you'll own your leadership.

Full Circle: Finding My Way Back to Me

At twenty-nine, I was fearless, knocking on doors, collecting no's and chasing yes's. Every rejection was fuel because I was getting closer to that "yes." Fast forward twenty years, and I've found that same fire again, but it burns steadier, wiser, and seasoned by scars and lessons that only time and experience can give.

This time, I'm not chasing achievements. I'm cultivating alignment. The truest blessing of my life has been peeling back the noise of expectation and choosing to live as the version of me that feels most real. The same boldness that pushed me through glass ceilings at twenty-nine now fuels how I flip the switch in culture. Leadership is about creating environments where others can find their own version of becoming.

Flipping the Switch on Culture

When I first stepped into senior leadership, it was a responsibility that went beyond being just "a role." I wasn't just inheriting a team or a title, but a culture that needed healing, rebuilding, and hope. Culture can weigh people down or set them free, and I wanted to be the kind of leader who made people feel lighter when they walked into work.

Coming out of the pandemic, that mission took on a whole new meaning. The world had been turned inside out. People were tired mentally, emotionally, and spiritually, and were faced with walking back into a workplace that no longer felt like home. The hallways were quieter, the smiles slower to appear, and looking people in the eyes somehow lost its groove. Behind every login and every camera lens, there was hesitation. And the only way forward was to rebuild trust one conversation, one connection, and one courageous act at a time.

So, I led differently. Instead of starting with performance metrics or compliance charts, I started with people. I traveled across the country—branch to branch, warehouse to warehouse—to just listen. I ditched the idea of a blazer and heels and showed up in steel-toed boots, a company jersey, and jeans, coffee in hand with my heart wide open. I asked real questions instead of polished and leading ones. What's working? What's not? What's breaking your spirit? And I listened to understand.

At first, there was hesitation. Trust had been bruised. But the more I listened, the more stories surfaced. They were raw, honest, and human.

And I, too, shared my own stories so the teams could know me. Slowly, the air shifted, and people exhaled.

Ideas started flowing. No one asked for miracles, but they asked to be heard. And we co-created solutions together that were practical, human, and possible.

Over time, the small acts of following up, following through, and naming the truth began to compound. Fear loosened its grip and courage stepped forward. People started showing up differently because they *wanted* to.

When members of the Global Executive Management Board later visited, one in particular looked around the room alive with open dialogue and realized he didn't need a slide deck. As they left later that day, he said, "You can feel it here. You've built something rare."

Culture, when it's real, doesn't need to be explained because it's *felt*.

GEM: Culture doesn't just happen because you design it. It happens because you live it, together, one choice at a time.

The Engagement Tour:
The *How* Behind the Feeling

The board reaction wasn't a surprise but the reflection of months of human work. Work that didn't start in a boardroom or behind a desk but on the ground and in the places where the heartbeat of our business really lives.

When I first set out on what would become known as *The Engagement Tour*, I had no fancy playbook, only a simple vision: to rebuild trust. I didn't want to talk about culture; I wanted to walk with it, to see it, hear the stories that didn't always make it to head office, and feel it up close.

So, I packed my bag and visited seventy-eight workshops over five months. Branch to branch, warehouse to warehouse, coast to coast. I went without slides and without scripts, just as a person connecting with other people. Every stop looked a little different—in shipping bays and boardrooms, in break areas and conference rooms—but the heart of what made the people feel fulfilled and respected was the same.

I showed up as Dianna, as a woman who wanted to listen, learn and lead differently, putting aside the title of "president." I sat at tables with dispatchers, coordinators, forklift drivers, sales teams, customer service professionals and operations managers. I asked them to tell me the truth, not what they thought I wanted to hear.

Instead of gathering ideas to send up the chain, I handed the power back to them. Every participant left with a 30-day personal commitment, one action they could take ownership of right away. These were our quick wins that didn't need approval and weren't limited by red tape. And we tracked every one of those commitments—over 1,500 in total—unlocking more than 5,000 opportunities for improvement. Some were small (adding water coolers or better lighting). Others were bold (cross-functional collaboration, automation, customer experience design). But regardless of the scale and scope, the real win wasn't the list itself but the lift it caused by engaging with each item on the list.

Word traveled fast, and before long, that energy became contagious. People started asking, "When's our session?" They didn't want to sit on the sidelines anymore; they wanted in.

While walking into a site after one of the first sessions, a warehouse professional came up to me with a smile. "Dianna, we actually did the thing we talked about." He walked me over to a newly organized space, explaining how they'd cut time off their process and made it safer for the team. The pride in his voice said everything about the level of empowerment that came with trusting them with accountability and ownership, and in return, offering the same the other way around.

From coast to coast, the conversations got deeper. Walls came down and hierarchies softened. The distance between frontlines and the boardroom began to close. People were no longer whispering frustrations behind closed doors but were problem-solving out loud. They were leading from wherever they stood.

By the end of the tour, I could feel the shift everywhere I went. The laughter in the hallways. The way people looked me in the eye again. The small but powerful spark of ownership that comes when people realize, I have a voice. That's what the Executive Board walked into later on, a culture in motion. A living breathing organization that remembered what it means to care, to connect, and to trust.

GEM: Culture moves at the speed of trust. And trust grows one honest conversation at a time.

Star Teams: Where Culture Takes Flight

Every culture shift needs a heartbeat, and for me, that heartbeat is the team. No single person carries culture. A star team isn't a collection of high performers, but a circle of high-performing humans connected by values and beliefs. They challenge each other to grow without competition. They hold each other accountable through honesty, empathy, reliability, and skill—the same anchors that built the H.E.R.S. model.

When I think about the star team we built, it was about harmony. We didn't need everyone to play the same instrument. We just needed each person to play their own, beautifully and in rhythm with the rest.

Building that kind of team takes time, trust, and truth-telling. It means no longer hiring for comfort and hiring instead for courage. It means you surround yourself with people who see your blind spots and love you enough to name them. A team of stars wins games, but a star team can change the game for everyone.

How It Started

When I first stepped into the role as president, I knew culture would only move if the people at the top lived it first. You can't build trust across an organization if it doesn't exist around your own table. So, I looked at my leadership team (brilliant, experienced, and passionate people) and asked, "Are we modeling the culture we're asking everyone else to build?"

The honest answer was, not yet. There were gaps in connection. We trusted each other's competence but not yet each other's vulnerability. The conversations were safe, structured, and polite but not real. So, we did the work together. We started having the conversations that most teams avoid; the kind that stretch you, humble you, and ultimately bond you. We built our own framework, called The Team Ten, a set of principles that guided how we'd show up together.

Team Ten

1. Always show up. These meetings are priority above all else.

2. Show-up prepared and fully engaged.

3. Listen before you defend.

4. Respect the pause. Not every silence needs to be filled.

5. Celebrate the win before chasing the next.

6. Handle conflict with courage instead of avoidance.

7. Make the decision; clear the parking lot.

8. Welcome new stars.

9. Honour the stars moving on.

10. Keep joy in the agenda. Laughter builds trust faster than meetings.

We didn't get it perfect every day, but we kept it honest and used our trust bank to showcase if we were adding to it or depleting it.

As our connection deepened and the energy around us started to shift. People could feel it. The trust that had been built around our table began to move outward through branches, regions, warehouses, and departments until it touched the farthest corners of the company.

The Art of Choosing Your Stars

Building a star team starts in a conversation. I meet candidates over coffee or tea, human to human. I ask questions that don't live on an HR checklist, and that'll travel through our conversation:

— What story have you had to unlearn about yourself?

— When was the last time you failed at something that mattered?

— What part of your professional identity is just armour?

I want to see who they are when no one is watching. Because leadership, at its core, is about character. And when finalists reach the last round, I never hire alone. We conduct a star-team interview for shared accountability. Authenticity and ego can't coexist for long in that space.

The Glue that Holds Us Together

Once the team is built, the real work begins. A star team isn't maintained by meetings or metrics. It lives and breathes through connection you can't fake; the kind built in the in-between moments (the hallway laughs, the late-night calls, the "I'm not okay" moments where everyone rallies).

Our strength became our honesty. We gave each other permission to be fully human, to celebrate wins, grieve losses, and even disagree with respect. That's the kind of connection that flows through an organization and makes people emulate what they feel.

When the Stars Move on

It would be lovely if star teams stayed together forever, but real leadership means letting people grow, even if that means they outgrow you. When a member moves on, it's a sign that your legacy is working, as they get to carry it forward into their next role. They carry the same heartbeat, the same trust, into their next chapter.

When you lead through mutual trust, you stop fearing turnover and instead focus on celebrating expansion. The goal should never be to keep people but to equip them. Give them the courage and skill to keep leading through example wherever they go.

GEM: A star team doesn't just change what's possible in an organization. It redefines what's possible for everyone who touches it.

Full Circle: The Culture Impact

Looking back on those moments of listening, learning, and leading, the faces became the headlines. The nod when someone finally felt safe enough to speak. The laughter returning to the quiet hallways. The spark that shone when people realized we *did this together*. Culture doesn't flip overnight. It bends slowly toward truth and shifts when someone chooses to stay curious instead of defensive. It grows when leaders lean in, instead of standing tall. And it lasts when a team learns to trust not just the process but also each other.

Flipping the switch on culture has nothing to do with the stage or strategy decks. It's about the everyday choices that build belonging. It's the way you say thank you after a tough day. It's asking, "How are you really?" and wanting the answer. It's showing up in our own messy, real way that gives everyone else permission to do the same.

Culture needs a heartbeat, not a campaign. And once you find it, protect it passionately.

Your Pocket Flip-Kit:
3 Culture Shifts That Stick

1. Lead from listening

Don't underestimate the power of showing up with a curious heart. Ask the question behind the question, the one that makes someone pause before they answer. That's where truth lives!

2. Empower, don't own

Give people permission to move the needle without waiting for approval. When ownership expands, innovation follows and so does trust.

3. Celebrate progress

Culture doesn't change in leaps; it changes in layers. Notice the quiet wins and name them. They're proof that the shift is happening even when it still feels slow.

> **GEM: The culture you build isn't defined by what you say in meetings. It's revealed by how people feel when those meetings end.**

Flip the Switch Moment

Grab your journal or a blank page and think of this reflection not as a to-do list but as a map or a living document that captures where your culture is today and where it needs to grow next.

Spark Questions:

— What part of your culture makes you proud?

— Where is trust starting to fray?

— What story are people telling about what it feels like to work here?

Write down three things that make people *want* to be part of your team. These are your culture magnets, the invisible forces that pull people in and make them stay.

Then, consider who are your culture carriers? These are the people who naturally lift others, build bridges, and embody what your organization stands for. Name them. Then invest in them. Trust them with the torch.

When you finish, step back and look at your map. Where are the gaps? Where's the energy? What's asking for your attention next?

Culture needs direction, not some false sense of perfection.

The Part I Almost Left Out

This chapter took the most courage to write. There were nights I sat staring at a blank page, remembering moments when the weight felt heavier than my confidence, times I overpromised or hurried past the pause that was asking me to listen longer, times when I wondered if I was enough for the role I'd stepped into.

Those memories could've stayed hidden, but they shaped me the most. Sometimes, leadership looks like sitting in the office at 9:00 p.m. with a cup of cold coffee still listening to someone who just needs to be heard. Sometimes, it's choosing humility over hurry or saying, "I don't know, but I'm here to find out with you." It's not about being the smartest person in the room, but the safest. It's about creating spaces where people can breathe again, where ideas can grow, and where trust—the quiet edge of real leadership—can finally take root.

Flipping the switch is a way of living, a promise to keep showing up, even when it's uncomfortable, because that's how we build the kind of culture we'd be proud to inherit and one day leave behind to be carried forward without us.

Stay inspired,

CHAPTER 12

No Permission Required

"Sometimes just being yourself is the radical act.
When you occupy spaces that weren't built for you,
your authenticity is your activism."
— *Elaine Welteroth*

GEM: Leadership comes down to showing up fully as yourself, living with purpose, and inspiring others to do the same.

You lit up the room with trust and culture. You've peeled back the layers of old stories, rebuilt trust from the inside out, and led from your truest self. You've learned to flip the switch with courage and presence and move from performing to being. Now, take back the pen. This is the final flip: from permission-seeking to permission-giving. There are no gatekeepers or hall passes. The life you're building answers to your values, not someone else's approval.

Your greatest unfinished project will always be you. Every day, you're shaping yourself through movement, sometimes through stillness and often through the moments that feel uncomfortable. Some days, you'll become more of who you are meant to be. Other days, you'll be letting go and undoing the pieces that no longer fit. Both are essential pieces of progress.

Your Story Counts

Look back at all your reflections and messy notes in your journal: this is your story. Your story is your receipts, the choices people can feel. You may suddenly feel like your career path looks a little different, or perhaps you've reconnected with a passion you thought was long gone, or possibly identified partnerships that will be the very thing that helps you persevere. Whatever it may be, notice how your story is taking shape.

Your story is the blueprint of your leadership. It shows how far you've come and who you've become. Your story is your brand. It's how you show up and how people experience you.

Your brand is your behaviour. Every decision, every promise, and every time you choose empathy over ego, that's your leadership showing its face. And the most beautiful thing about this journey is that you are the architect. You decide how it's built and how it feels when people encounter it.

Your story is yours, exclusively. You may not love every chapter in your story. Some parts could be rewritten; others may bring your pride. But every single one of them matters. The messy pages hold the wisdom, and the mistakes hold the muscle. The heartbreaks hold your humanity and keep you real. And when you share those lessons, when you dare to say, "This is what I've lived, this is what I've learned," you give others permission to do the same.

Before you move forward, take a moment to honour the people who've walked beside you. The ones who saw you before you saw yourself. The ones who stayed when it was hard, and who believed in you even in those "what was I thinking" moments. Those people are part of your story too and who shaped your courage, stretched your heart, and helped you find your way back home to yourself. Text them one line today: *You helped me become.*

When you start to see the people who helped you rise, you notice the spaces that invite you to rise even higher.

Three Days That Changed Me

Years ago, at a three-day retreat, the agenda looked ordinary on paper, but the outcome wasn't. To my surprise, every person on the guest list was a woman. It was the first time the company had ever done something like that, and the energy in the room felt different: curious, a little cautious, but quietly electric.

On the second day, the facilitator handed out a sheet with three words at the top: *My River Story.* She asked us to trace the story of our life from the moment we were born to now, as if it were a river. We were told to go off alone, find a quiet corner, and spend three uninterrupted hours reflecting, drawing, and writing our story.

Three hours? I almost talked myself out of it. Then the river started talking back, and before I knew it, the story poured out.

At first, my river flowed gently. My childhood memories, moments of joy and early ambition. Then came the bends, the floods, and the rapids that tested my strength and pulled me under. The times when I had to rebuild, reinvent, and rediscover who I was meant to be. I traced every twist and current until the large flip-chart paper was full—and so was I.

When we gathered again as a group, what started as a leadership exercise became a moment of truth. Women began sharing their rivers, stories of survival, heartbreak, illness, fortitude, and hope. Some spoke through tears, others through laughter. Every river was different, but the sea was the same.

That day changed how I lead. Leadership didn't start when I had answers but when I let myself be seen. Strength isn't found by holding everything together. It's found by allowing yourself to be seen fully, imperfectly, and honestly. That's where empathy and trust are born, and that's where leadership begins.

When I brought My River Story home, I shared it with my husband and daughter. I laughed as I unfolded the page (my artistic skills leaving much to be desired), but the story was there, alive in every line I'd drawn. For the first time, my life made sense as a journey instead of some kind of checklist. It became something I could own, and something worth sharing.

I didn't realize it at the time, but that river became a mirror, one I still return to today.

No Permission Required

Your river story is yours alone. It twists, it bends, it slows, and it surges. It carries your values, your lessons, your pain, your pride, and every ounce of strength that brought you here. You're here because you overcame all of it and still rose.

What I learned from that experience was that I don't need permission to own my story. I don't need permission to tell it, live it, or lead it either. And neither do you.

When you embrace your story, when you truly stop editing yourself to fit into systems or expectations, you step into the current of your real power. That's where your authenticity lives. That's where leadership begins to feel effortless and R.E.A.L. because it's aligned.

Own the current. Drop the mask. Lead as you without requiring permission.

Your Pocket Flip-Kit: No Permission Required

1. Own your story

Stop self-editing yourself to fit smaller rooms. Every twist, detour, and imperfect moment has taught you something vital. Your story isn't your resume; it's your proof of courage. Tell it. Live it.

2. Flow with it

Rivers bend and so do seasons. When the waters feel rough, remember that the calm is coming, and when things are calm, remember you earned it. The current doesn't ask for permission to move, and neither should you.

3. Lead from within

Titles are optional; values aren't. When you lead with purpose, people find the light.

Look at the river of your life and choose one value that's carried you this far. How will you honour that value in the next season of your story? Write one simple promise to yourself—and sign it. That's your commitment to keep flowing forward.

GEM: You are the switch. Keep flipping it for yourself, for those who follow, and for the story still waiting to be written.

Flip the Switch Moment

Find a quiet space. Get a big paper or journal and draw your life as a river, from birth to now. If it gets heavy, pause and breathe.

Serenity (Still water)

When were the moments in your life when things truly felt calm and aligned, like you were exactly where you were meant to be? What were you doing during these times? Who was around you? What did those moments teach you?

> *Flip tips:* These calm, peaceful moments often uncover what grounds you. They can reveal your core values—like family, faith, or well-being—because serenity usually comes when you're aligned with what matters most. For example, sitting at a cottage with loved ones might uncover that connection or that mutual trust is a non-negotiable value for you.

Abundance (Flow)

These are times of growth and opportunity. When did you feel full? At these times, you may have experienced incredible energy, learning about new opportunities and overflowing possibilities. What were you building or discovering about you at this time? How did you show up? What strengths did you uncover? Who did you share this time with?

Flip tips: These are seasons when you feel energized and overflowing with possibility. They uncover your strengths and superpowers (what you're naturally great at when you're "in the flow"). For example, a career growth spurt could uncover values of inspiration or creativity or show you that you thrive when you're building something new.

Rapids (Tests)

Remember the tough and turbulent stretches of your life. What were the moments where you were tested? Maybe it was your perseverance or your patience being tested. How did you get through the chaos? What helped you keep your head above water? Or what did you learn from sinking?

Flip tips: These turbulent moments test your fortitude. They uncover how you cope under pressure and what internal tools you rely on. For example, a tough custody battle may uncover deep reserves of persistence and a value for family.

Floods (Overwhelm)

These were the times where you were incredibly overwhelmed with emotions or circumstances facing you head-on. When did life feel like it was too much? When were you emotionally, mentally, or physically in overload? What did you learn? How did those times shape your empathy or your perspective of you?

Flip tips: These overwhelming times uncover your emotional triggers and your empathy. They often shape your perspective, showing where you need boundaries or where compassion for yourself and others grows. For example, losing loved ones may uncover the value of joy or legacy because you see more clearly what you want to carry forward.

Rocks (Obstacles)

These are the obstacles you've run into that formed who you are today. What were the challenges that forced you to grow? What were the experiences when you felt incredibly uncomfortable? How did they strengthen you or your leadership? How did they increase your self awareness? What values surfaced during these moments?

Flip tips: These obstacles or naysayers reveal what you will and won't tolerate. They uncover your values by showing you what gets "triggered" and how you choose to respond. For example, a toxic colleague might uncover a value for respect and push you to develop tools like curiosity and pause before reacting.

Droughts (Dry Spells)

These are your dry spells. Longing for water (or something stronger) with not an ounce of liquid in sight. When did you feel stuck or disconnected? What helped you push through it? What did you discover in the stillness? How did these moments shift your priorities or shine a light on a new focus for your future?

Flip tips: These dry, empty stretches uncover your stamina and courage. They often highlight what truly fuels you because you feel the sharpness of its absence. For example, being a parent may uncover sacrifice and responsibility, showing that your persistence is rooted in love.

Riverbank (Perspective)

These are the times when you hit the pause button and observed. When did you take time to step back from it all, either by choice or by circumstance? What did you notice from the sidelines? How did that distance help you see things differently?

Flip tips: These pauses, when you step back to observe, uncover wisdom and perspective. They can reveal the importance of mentorship, reflection, or mutual trust. For example, watching your parents' or partner's example may uncover values you aspire to live by and pass forward… or not.

Step back. Notice the patterns: values that repeat, lessons that are calling, themes that refuse to be quiet. Those are your anchors. Name them.

GEM: Your river story is yours to own. Flow with it, live it, and lead it without needing permission.

A Love Letter to Becoming

I wrote this chapter for myself. For the woman who tried to be everything for everyone; for the leader who pushed so hard, she forgot to breathe; for the human who finally learned that grace is wisdom instead of weakness.

Writing this and reminiscing about my own river was raw, like sitting beside my own river, watching the currents I once fought so hard to control finally find their rhythm. I saw the floods that once broke me now feeding something stronger. I saw the calm waters I used to take for granted and realized they were moments that healed me.

Somewhere along the way, I stopped chasing and started listening. I realized that every version of me—the brave one, the tired one, and the unfinished one—deserved a place in the story.

This chapter is also a love letter to every part of you that's still learning, still flowing, and still finding its way home. You're allowed to be a masterpiece and a work-in-progress at the same time.

GEM: The most powerful story you'll ever tell is the one you finally allow yourself to live.

So, before we close this journey together, take one last look at your river, and see not what's missing but what's already flowing within you.

From the 6Ps to R.E.A.L. to H.E.R.S., you've built the muscle, the method, and the mirror. The conclusion will hand you the keys to keep the switch on without apology.

Stay inspired,

Flip the Switch... and Leave It On

> *"Success is not final, failure is not fatal; it is the*
> *courage to continue that counts"*
> —*Winston Churchill*

GEM: The flip may be momentary, but the staying power is what changes outcomes.

You've done so much more than read a book. You've learned how to turn courage into flow and purpose into power. Every time you chose courage over comfort, every time you leaned into truth instead of hiding behind safety, you flipped the switch—and kept the light on. Every reflection, every pause, every "aha" moment you've had along the way has sparked something lasting, and that spark is now yours to carry forward.

Growth always stretches before it strengthens. But when your purpose is clear, you'll see how validation loses its pull. You'll stop chasing applause and start creating impact. That's when leadership becomes a light that stops flickering, burning steady and strong.

In a world that rewards conformity and "sameness," you've chosen authenticity. In a culture that rewards performance, you've chosen purpose. And that one act—the choice to stop playing it safe—is your competitive edge. And flipping the switch on your own light gives everyone around you permission to shine, too.

When things get uncertain (and they will), remember that you're not doing this alone. Your inner cabinet, your trusted circle, is your grounding wire. They remind you of who you are when the noise gets loud. And together, you don't just survive the dark. That's H.E.R.S. in action and practiced in community.

When you turned the first few pages of *Flip the Switch*, I promised to bring your potential to the very top of your priority list, to help you uncover your unique superpowers, and to give you a system to create consistent, meaningful breakthroughs. My hope was that you feel the shift now that we've reached the end, not just in your thinking but in your confidence, energy, and belief in what's possible for you.

You've walked through the 6Ps. You've learned how to keep it R.E.A.L. and that building mutual trust is the heartbeat of leadership. You've seen that authenticity requires your being in motion. You've seen how the old story of "I'm not enough" can be replaced with "I was made for this!" You've collected GEMs that lit my path, and I hope they'll keep lighting up yours.

But the end of this book isn't the end of our journey. It's merely your ignition point. You now carry the tools, the truth, and the awareness to turn intention into action, fear into fuel, and potential into performance.

The most remarkable journey of your life isn't the one you've just read but the one you'll write next. Your next level isn't waiting somewhere out there; it's already burning inside you.

Stop demanding permission from yourself and the universe to flip the switch. Just do it. Live it. Lead it. And whatever you do, leave it on.

GEM: The choices you make today are the bridge to who you're becoming.

Keep it R.E.A.L. Keep the switch turned on. Stay inspired, always.

A heartfelt acknowledgement goes to...

My husband, Stephene, who's my greatest ally, my quiet strength, and the steady heartbeat behind every chapter of this book. You've been beside me in every season—in love, leadership, parenting, and purpose. You've walked with me through the unglamorous middle (the messy drafts, the late-night edits, and the moments when I wasn't sure I had the words left to give). You've read every chapter more times than I can count, always finding meaning I didn't even know I'd written. You've uncovered hidden GEMs, lifted my voice when it wavered, and helped me see the story within the story.

You're my safe space and my mirror, the one who calls me higher while keeping me grounded. Through this journey, you've reminded me what partnership really means.

You believed in *Flip the Switch* before it ever had a title. You believed in me before I fully believed in myself. And through that belief, you gave me the courage to lead, to write, and live wide open and without permission.

This book carries your fingerprints in the encouragement whispered across the kitchen counter, the laughter that broke through long writing days, and the countless moments when your patience made space for my purpose. My love for you is immeasurable because of who you are, not what you do for me. You're my home in the truest sense of the word.

Thank you for standing beside me in every chapter of our life together.

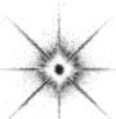

My parents, who were my very first teachers in what it means to lead with heart.

Mom, you taught me what perseverance really sounds like. From the piano bench where I learned to practice through every wrong note to the moments when life itself felt out of tune, you showed me the beauty of persistence. You never stopped playing, even when it hurt, even when it was hard, even when no one was listening. You taught me that the magic isn't in the performance but the practice and in the grace to begin again.

Dad, you were my teacher long before I ever stepped into a classroom, and my coach long after the final inning. On the baseball field, you taught me about focus, discipline, and teamwork; in life, you taught me about character, humility, and heart. You showed me that leadership is about setting the tone through consistency and care. You believed in me before I fully believed in myself, and you pushed me to keep swinging, even when I struck out.

Together, you've built the foundation of who I am. You gave me equal parts of grit and grace and the belief that no matter how hard the game, it should be played with integrity, empathy, and heart.

Every word in *Flip the Switch* carries a piece of you both; the lessons, the laughter, and the love that shaped how I lead and who I'm still becoming. You lit the first switch in me and taught me to keep it burning bright.

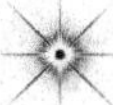

My Auntie Mary and Godfather Uncle David, my steady light and safe harbour. You've been there through some of my darkest hours, standing quietly in faith when words were hard to find and celebrating every bright chapter with joy felt like family multiplied. You've cheered me on from the sidelines, prayed me through storms, and wrapped my husband and daughter in love as if they were your own.

Your faith has always been my reminder that grace is fierce and that prayer is not just something we whisper but something we practice with trust, patience, and purpose. You've shown me that sometimes leadership isn't about standing in front but standing beside. And that kind of presence is the truest form of mutual trust.

In many ways, this book exists because of you. Your belief in me was a bridge back to myself when I forgot where the shore was. Your encouragement helped me keep the light on when the path felt dim. You reminded me that faith and persistence are my companions.

Thank you for loving us as your own, for the prayers that lifted me higher than I knew I could reach, and for being the kind of leaders who lead through faith, humility, and heart. I'm endlessly grateful to be part of your story, just as you've been such a beautiful part of mine.

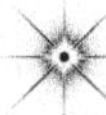

My inner cabinet, my closest friends and confidants, you have been with me through it all, and your unwavering support has been my lifeline. You've been the gentle push when I hesitated and the voice of reason when I couldn't see my way forward. As I've traveled through my river of life, your belief in me has been like a lighthouse cutting through the fog and guiding me when I've felt lost. The encouragement and laughs we've shared have brought me so much joy! And the moments of quiet understanding have been permanently ingrained in me with a love and strength I carry with me.

I am who I am today because you chose to show up for me every time I asked and even when I didn't. As I continue to navigate my river of life, I carry your spirit with me, knowing that we can weather any storm and celebrate every success while in the flow together.

Thank you for being the heart and soul of my story. Your impact is immeasurable, and my gratitude runs deep.

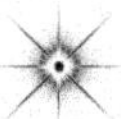

My Star Team, during the time of writing this book, have been my greatest allies, my solid advocates of flipping the switch, and true partners in bringing these concepts to life in our business. Whether it was building a connected culture rooted in psychological safety and trust, leading engagement with heart and hustle, collaborating and creating strong visibility in the market, showing up consistently as your authentic selves in every situation we entered, or continuously finding new ways to innovate and test our growth mindset as a team, we've done all of it together.

This book is a tribute to your leadership and your trust in making our connected and empowering culture the one certainty our people can count on. I'm deeply grateful and will forever be inspired by you.

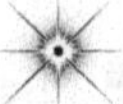

My colleagues across Kuehne + Nagel Canada, thank you. You're the heartbeat behind every lesson, every story, and every spark within these pages. You've shown me, time and again, what it means to lead with courage, grace, and grit. You've created an environment where trust is lived instead of merely being spoken and a magical space where ideas thrive, voices are heard, and growth is a shared journey.

It's been one of the greatest privileges of my career to serve and learn alongside you, to witness firsthand how culture moves, how connection deepens, and how a team built on mutual trust can truly change what's possible. You've taught me that leadership is a symphony requiring many people. And because of you, I've had the chance to flip the switch repeatedly and to keep it lit.

To every warehouse, every branch and boardroom, thank you for the laughter, the hard conversations, the late nights, the learning, and the courage to keep it R.E.A.L.

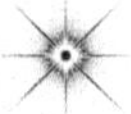

And finally, to my employer, **Kuehne + Nagel International AG,** I'm honoured to lead within an organization that's not only embraced my leadership but actively created the space for me to thrive in my truth. Just as people grow, evolve, and learn to flip the switch, so do great organizations. Kuehne + Nagel has demonstrated the courage to lean into transformation, and I'm proud to help lead that charge here in Canada.

This is a company grounded in purpose and powered by possibility, and I couldn't be prouder to represent a global business that's bold and dynamic with a vision to become the most trusted supply chain partner, supporting a sustainable future.

About the Author

Dianna Fioravanti is a trailblazing executive, leadership mentor, and motivational speaker who believes real leadership begins the moment you stop playing it safe.

As President of Kuehne+Nagel Canada, she leads one of the world's most respected logistics organizations and made history as the first woman to hold this role in the company's Canadian history. Over her 25-year career, she has led with courage, care, and candor—building trust, connection, and authenticity while inspiring teams to deliver exceptional results.

Under her leadership, Kuehne+Nagel Canada has earned multiple Great Place to Work honours, including Best Workplaces Led by Women and Best Workplaces in Transportation & Logistics, as well as recognition for its Most Trusted Executive Team.

In 2025, Dianna was named a Woman of Inspiration, receiving the *Women in Power* Award from the Universal Women's Network. She also earned the Certified Canadian Logistics Management Professional (CCLMP) designation from CITT, reinforcing her commitment to excellence in her field and lifelong learning.

Her defining turning point came from an unexpected source—her daughter—who once called her dreams "boring." That moment flipped a switch. Dianna realized she'd been living small inside a life that no longer fit. She left the safety of a long-standing insurance career and stepped boldly into an unfamiliar industry, turning that leap into a powerful chapter of reinvention and leadership.

Today, Dianna helps leaders at every level rediscover their courage, claim their voice, and lead from their own playbook. She is passionate about transforming self-doubt into conviction and authenticity into a superpower.

A proud Canadian, Dianna holds an Honours degree in Political Science from the University of Waterloo, the Chartered Insurance Professional (CIP) designation, and completed the Senior Leader Executive Program at Cranfield University in the United Kingdom.

When she's not leading, writing, or speaking, she's traveling with her husband, exploring new destinations, or enjoying life at home in Kitchener-Waterloo—golfing, reading, and sharing good food and laughter with loved ones.

Her guiding motto is one she lives deeply: **"The greatest unfinished project you'll ever work on is you."** Because at the end of every chapter—every risk, every reinvention—there is one truth she hopes every reader remembers: **your switch flips the moment you choose yourself.**

Bibliography:

Bagehot, Walter. 2023. *Estimates of Some Englishmen and Scotchmen.* N.p.: Salzwasser-Verlag.

Churchill, Winston, and Fred R. Shapiro. 2021. *The New Yale Book of Quotations.* New Haven, CT: Yale University Press.

Coelho, Paulo. n.d. "Paul Coelho Quotes," Attributed quote to Coelho, resonates with themes found in his published works. https://www.goodreads.com/quotes/7634880-maybe-the-journey-isn-t-so-much-about-becoming-anything-maybe.

Covey, Stephen R. 1989. *The Seven Habits of Highly Effective People.* New York, New York: Simon and Schuster.

Einhorn, Cheryl S. 2025. "In Uncertain Times, Ask These Questions Before You Make a Decision." In Uncertain Times, Ask These Questions Before You Make a Decision. https://hbr.org/2025/05/in-uncertain-times-ask-these-questions-before-you-make-a-decision.

Einstein, Albert. 2024. "26 Brilliant Albert Einstein Quotes | Quotes from Albert Einstein." Reader's Digest. https://www.rd.com/article/albert-einstein-quotes/.

Gerstner, Louis V. 2003. *Who Says Elephants Can't Dance? Leading a Great Enterprise Through Dramatic Change*. N.p.: HarperCollins.

Gitomer, Jeffrey. 2023. *Jeffrey Gitomer's Little Red Book of Selling: 12.5 Principles of Sales Greatness. How to Make Sales Forever*. N.p.: Sound Wisdom.

Graziosi, Dean. 2019. *Millionaire Success Habits: The Gateway to Wealth & Prosperity*. Carlsbad, California: Hay House.

Gretzky, Wayne. n.d. Quote Inspired by his father, Walter Gretzky. In *Wayne Gretzky Quotes*. Goodreads. https://www.goodreads. com/author/quotes/240132.Wayne_Gretzky.

Jordan, Michael. n.d. "Michael Jordan - Some people want it to happen, some wish…" Brainy Quote. Accessed September 28, 2025. https://www.brainyquote.com/quotes/ michael_jordan_167382.

King Jr., Martin L. 1954. "Rediscovering Lost Values," Sermon. The Martin Luther King Jr., Research and Education Institute. https://kinginstitute.stanford.edu/king-papers/documents/ rediscovering-lost-values-0.

Loder, Sandy. 2023. "The impact of 45,000 negative thoughts, Sandy Loder." Peak Dynamics. https:// insights.peak-dynamics.net/post/102ia4i/ the-impact-of-45-000-negative-thoughts#menu-navmain.

Macdonald, George. 2024. *The Marquis of Lossie*. N.p.: Repro India Limited.

McConaughey, Matthew. 2020. *Greenlights*. N.p.: Crown.

Nightingale, Earl. 1956. *The Strangest Secret*. N.p.: Rough Draft Printing.

Obama, Michelle. 2018. "Becoming by Michelle Obama." Michelle Obama Books. https://michelleobamabooks.com/becoming/.

Peale, Norman V. 2022. *A Guide to Confident Living*. N.p.: Simon & Schuster Audio.

Robbins, Tony. 2024. "Where focus goes, energy flows." Tony Robbins. https://www.tonyrobbins.com/blog/where-focus-goes-energy-flows?

Thatcher, Margaret. 1965. "Speech to National Union of Townswomen's Guilds Conference." Margaret Thatcher Foundation. https://www.margaretthatcher.org.

Welteroth, Elaine. 2019. *More Than Enough: Claiming Space for Who You Are (No Matter What They Say)*. N.p.: Penguin Publishing Group.

Yeung, Anthony J. 2022. "One Little Thing That's Blocking Your Success: Envy." Medium. https://medium.com/mind-cafe/one-little-thing-thats-blocking-your-success-envy-c99c34e7ab31.

Keep the Switch On - Let's Grow Together

You've started something powerful. By reading *Flip the Switch*, you've already taken the brave step from playing it safe to crushing it. Now, let's keep the momentum alive.

Join me as we keep building what you've begun:

Executive mentorship: Personalized. Transformational. R.E.A.L. Go deeper into your leadership, your purpose, and your potential. Together, we'll design a path that's authentic, aligned, and built to last and that reflects the leader you are and the one you're still becoming.

Keynotes that move people: Bring me to your next event, and let's unleash what's possible; storytelling, strategy, and soul that turn inspiration to action. Because when we connect heart to strategy, real change happens.

A community that rises together: Step into a circle of heart-led leaders who are flipping the switch every day with R.E.A.L. conversations, support, and growth.

Connect & Collaborate

Visit <u>www.diannafioravanti.com</u> to explore how we can partner through mentorship, special events, podcasts, and curated experiences for you and your team.

However we connect, let's co-create the next chapter of your story and keep the momentum alive. Because when you keep the switch on, you don't just change what's possible for yourself. You also change what's possible for everyone around you.

GEM: The flip starts with you, but the momentum multiplies when we rise together.

URGENT PLEA!

Thank you for reading my book!

I really appreciate all of your feedback and

I love hearing what you have to say.

I need your input to make the next version of this

book (and my future books) better.

If this book flipped even *one* switch for you,

please take 2 minutes to leave a review on Amazon.

Your words help someone else find the
courage to stop playing it safe.

Thank you for being part of this movement.

Stay Inspired,

Dianna